removing spots and stains

IBERT MELLAN, PH.G., M.S.
Director of Research, Polychrome Corporation

AND

ELEANOR MELLAN, PH.G.
Librarian

1959

chemical publishing co., inc.
212 fifth avenue, new york, n. y.

Removing Spots and Stains

© 2011 by Chemical Publishing Co., Inc. All rights reserved. This book is protected by copyright. No part of it may be reproduced, stored in a retrieval system or transmitted in any form or by any means; electronic, mechanical, photocopying, recording or otherwise, without the prior written permission of the publisher.

ISBN: 978-0-8206-0032-1

Chemical Publishing Company:
www.chemical-publishing.com
www.chemicalpublishing.net

First edition:
© Chemical Publishing Company, Inc. – New York, 1959
Second Impression:
Chemical Publishing Company, Inc. - 2011

Printed in the United States of America

contents

	Preface	5
Chapter	1. Introduction	7
	2. Fibers	10
	3. Fabrics	21
	4. Dyes	29
	5. Basic Rules for Stain Removal	33
	6. Safety Rules to Insure Best Results	35
	7. Equipment Aids to Stain Removal	36
	8. Stain Removing Agents	38
	9. Stains and Methods for Their Removal	40

preface

Home care requires the utmost skill and ingenuity of the homemaker. Because of the extremely high standard of dress and personal hygiene in this country, endless care and effort is expended in order to maintain this acute attention to good grooming. For the homemaker, the removal of stains represents a major portion of her expertness in running her home successfully. Each member of her family contributes his and her share of stains not only in the natural use of their surroundings, but more often in their use of wearing apparel. The frequent need for removing stains from clothing bears heavily upon the budget where one is completely dependent upon professional cleaning. To meet this challenge, the thrifty and efficient homemaker seeks information and the means by which she can care for garments, household linen, and household furnishings.

The professional cleaner is equally alert in keeping abreast with information that concerns his work and efficiency. Textile fabrics are of the greatest variety and complexity in their chemical and physical composition. Also the stains are often complex in nature since a stain may be composed of several staining substances such as, for example, machine oil which in addition to the oil, may contain particles of metal and carbon. The dry cleaner in the end is sought for his special skill and experience in dealing with complex stains and for the reconditioning of a fabric as near as possible to its original physical condition and appearance.

This book is designed to present basic facts and give simple rules and directions for the use of the homemaker who can then remove spots and stains effectively and economically. The book also affords the dry cleaner with a ready reference to the stain removing chemicals and the procedures in applying them. The dry cleaning industry and allied industries where spot and stain removal are of interest, should welcome an up-to-date and simplified treatment of this subject which includes information on the newer fibers, fabrics, and dyes.

CHAPTER 1

introduction

Several primary rules are given in the following text which when remembered and applied before proceeding with the task of stain removal, gives the user increased assurance of success. Methods are also given for preparing the agents necessary in stain removal thus making it possible to construct a kit which can provide the quick, ready and convenient means of dealing with the removal of stains.

Prompt Removal

Prompt removal of a stain is of primary importance. Time often determines how easily a stain can be removed. The chances of complete removal lessen as time goes by, and old stains are sometimes impossible to remove.

Identify the Nature of Your Fabric

Is the cloth made of rayon, cotton, silk, wool, nylon, vinyon, or any one of the new synthetic fibers or combinations of these, which are steadily flowing into the textile market?

What Is the Nature of the Stain?

Much guessing can be eliminated by a familiarity with the appearance of many of the common stains, such as general soil, ink, fruit, sugar, grease, cod-liver oil, automobile grease, salad dressing, etc. A clue to its identity is often provided by the appearance, feel, smell, and color of a stain. Grease usually produces a dark semitransparent stain. A grease stain on household linen set by laundering is usually dark brown. Fruit stains vary in color; syrups produce a stiff sugary stain which, when scratched, will turn white; light-brown or tan stains are generally due to coffee, tea, and cocoa. Brown stains very often are due to tannin. A black shiny stain usually turns out to be caused by pitch, paint, or oxidized, heavy road oil. Liquors, beer, perfume, disinfectants can usually be identified by their odors.

Careful Treatment

Careful treatment is the best approach to a stain. Work lightly and rapidly. Vigorous rubbing is often fatal to the cloth, its color, or its finish.

Give Your Stain Remover Time to Act

Your spot remover, whether it is a solvent, lubricant, or softening agent, enzymic digestant, etc., should be given time in which to exert its action on the stain.

Test Your Stain Removers

Test your stain removers on an inconspicuous spot, such as an unexposed seam or hem. Observe whether it injures the color or dye, or the fiber of the garment. It is best to be cautious rather than sorry. It is necessary sometimes to face the choice between a stain on your garment or a faded or otherwise injured spot.

Determine Whether Your Cloth Is Washable or Nonwashable

This information is highly useful in simplifying your task. A tag or label may reveal this information or, if this is lacking, you may consider it washable if it has been previously washed successfully.

Consider Simple Methods First

Simple methods often prove effective. A nongreasy stain may disappear when sponged with cold water. It is wise to test the cloth first to be sure that water does not cause it to "water spot." Grease stains will frequently respond effectively to a grease solvent, such as V.M. & P. naphtha, which is a safe solvent and, therefore, to be recommended. Be sure, however, to use this solvent far from an open fire and refrain from smoking during its use. Hot water will set many stains and its use should be avoided when the nature of the stain is unknown.

Introduction

Use Stain Removers Sparingly

Be sparing in the use of a stain remover. Better results are obtained by many short applications than one long one.

Use Light Brushing Motions

Light brushing motions should be used, starting well outside the stain and brushing toward the center. This lessens the possibility of being left with grease rings. This inward brushing is also known and described as "feathering out."

Flush Out the Stain Remover

Flush out well any chemical which has been used for the purpose of neutralizing acid or alkaline stains. Avoid the use of strong acids and alkalies which weaken your cloth.

Dry Rapidly

The treated area should be permitted to dry rapidly. In this way, damage due to prolonged action of the solvent is avoided. It should also be remembered that rayon fibers are weaker when wet than when dry.

CHAPTER 2

fibers

The modern textile industry presents a complex picture in which the old natural fibers are now blended with many new synthetic fibers and in many instances are entirely replaced by them. It is now possible to make these new fibers assume the appearance of silk, wool, linen, etc. This points clearly to the necessity of testing a fabric to learn its composition and thus to be guided in selecting the cleaning chemicals and cleaning methods which can be safely followed in the removal of spots and stains. In the description of fibers which follows, a few of the simpler reactions of textile fibers to acids, alkalies, cleaning solvents, bleaches, and mechanical action have been included.

When cleaning a fabric, our first thought is to preserve as far as possible its original color. We can do this only by proceeding with caution and testing the effect of our cleaning substance on an unexposed area of the garment. The need for this precaution becomes apparent when we realize that the cleaning solvent which may be an acid, alkali, bleach, etc., may be an excellent choice for removing the offending stain but may at the same time cause either a loss of color, or bleeding of the color, or even destroy the fabric itself. The sizings and finishes used in a fabric must also guide us in our choice of cleaners and the methods used for this task.

The textile fabrics that are familiar to most of us are the natural fabrics made from cotton, linen, silk, and wool, and the synthetic rayon and nylon which have been available to us for some time. There are also newer synthetic fabrics, such as Orlon, Dacron, Dynel, Vicara, and others.

Silk

Silk is an animal product made from the spun threads of the silk worm which it processes to form its cocoon. There are two types of silk: One is produced by the cultivated silk worm which feeds on mulberry leaves and makes a white silk, and the other is made by the wild silk worm which feeds on wild vegetation and forms a darker and coarser silk which we know as shantungs, pongees, and tussahs.

There are synthetic silklike fabrics on the market and fabrics made of silk blended with other fibers. These different varieties of fabrics have different physical and chemical properties and there is a need for testing the fabric before removing stains. This can be done with a fair degree of accuracy by the simple burning test.

Pure silk will burn much like wool, but more rapidly giving off both a sizzling sound and an odor of burning feathers. Little shiny beads of ash are formed which powder more easily and quickly than wool ash and are also lighter and a bit softer. Vegetable synthetic fibers such as cellulose acetate rayon, burn more quickly than silk and without its frying action. The ash beads of cellulose acetate do not crush as easily when pressed with the fingers.

A further test may be made by examining the warp and weft threads of the fabric under an ordinary magnifying glass. Some fine silk fabrics are woven spirally around a cotton thread and this can be seen by fraying an end of the thread and examining under the magnifying glass.

Although weighted silk has almost disappeared in recent years, an old garment may still remain in your possession which is made of weighted silk. Weighting was done with metallic salts, such as of tin. These, in a burning test, will burn slowly without forming an ash and will glow much like the filament in an electric bulb. The metallic residue is not easily separated from the unburned fabric. Weighted silk can also be detected by its tendency to split along straight lines when rubbed vigorously. The burning test will give a sufficient clue since weighted silk is never mixed with other fibers. Test your stain-removing solvent before using on weighted silk to make sure that it is not harmful to the weighting material used.

Although silk is considered one of the strongest of fibers, a fabric made of silk may not be subjected to more hard rubbing or manipulation than other fabrics since its strength is dependent on its weave and the content of silk fiber.

Silk is destroyed by hot and concentrated solutions of strong alkalies, but weak, cool solutions of an alkali, such as ammonia water can be used with comparative safety. Of the organic and mineral acids made available for stain removal, only cool and very dilute solutions can be used successfully on silk. A dilute solution of acetic acid is safe to use and has the advantage of evaporating completely from the fabric.

Heat is injurious to animal fibers and, therefore, hot treatments for stain removal or pressing silk fabric with a hot iron should be avoided.

Although there are some bleaches that may be used safely on silk, avoid the use of sodium hypochlorite bleaches, since these destroy animal fibers.

Perspiration is destructive to silk because of the salt which is an important ingredient of perspiration and which is harmful to this fiber.

Wool

Wool is an animal or protein material which comes from the coats of sheep and goats. The fiber is composed of horny scales which may be seen under a magnifying glass. Since many synthetic fibers are made to resemble wool, it is advisable to learn the true nature of your cloth. A burning test can be made on a small clip of the cloth or even a few strands of fiber. Put a lighted match to it and if your test material is wool, it will burn slowly with a sputtering action, leaving a dry gray or black ash which does not smoulder nor glow when the flame is removed. It gives off an odor of burning hair. Other fibers such as rayon or cotton, when mixed with wool, will reveal their presence by burning more quickly, will sputter less and leave a smaller quantity of ash. The flame is yellow and when the light is removed, the fibers are likely to smoulder.

Wool is a stronger fiber than silk but it cannot be subjected to an overly severe rubbing or mechanical action because there is the risk of felting the fabric. This injury cannot be remedied.

Being an animal fiber, hot cleaning solutions cannot be used and pressing with a hot iron must be avoided. It is possible to use cold dilute solutions of mineral acids successfully, but hot concentrated solutions must be avoided. It is best to avoid the use of most alkalies which will attack wool more readily than acids. A dilute solution of ammonia water, however, may be used because of its mildness and its ability to evaporate completely from the cloth. Any yellowing that is evident when ammonia water is used indicates the need of neutralizing with a dilute solution of acetic acid. As with silk, avoid the use of hypochlorite bleaches.

Cotton and Linen

Cotton and linen are cellulose fibers obtained from plants and their reactions when treated with stain removers, are practically the same.

Fibers

These fibers will yellow when exposed to light for a long period and the most satisfactory means of treating this condition is by washing with soap and water.

Cotton fabric is usually cleaned and spots are removed by the familiar use of soap and water. However, cottons are not always found as such today since they are frequently blended with synthetic fibers, such as cellulose acetate rayon or other rayons and even with the natural fibers of silk and wool. Here again we may resort to a burning test which can quickly reveal the presence of cotton.

Cotton burns quickly with a yellow flame, giving off an odor of burning paper or wood. The fiber smoulders after removing the flame and its ash is light and fluffy, floating off in little flakes.

Linen burns much like cotton, but it will smoulder a longer time than cotton after removing the flame, and the color of its ash is found to be gray to black. The ash, too, is lighter in weight than the cotton ash.

To test for a starch finish, apply a drop of water to the fabric. If starch is present, the water spreads rapidly in all directions.

Cotton and linen can be treated safely with dilute solutions of organic acids, such as acetic acid. However, inorganic acids, such as hydrochloric or sulfuric acid, are injurious and only very dilute solutions may be used. Even such mild acids as lemon juice or vinegar can prove to be harmful when permitted to remain on the cloth for too long a time. Linen and cotton, however, show more resistance to alkalies and, unlike silk and wool, are safely treated with sodium hypochlorite bleach which is the most frequently used bleach for these fibers. Dilute solutions of ammonia water, washing or baking soda may also be used, but it is important to wash out these alkalies as quickly and thoroughly as possible.

Synthetic Fibers

The modern textile industry has expanded so remarkably within recent years that the natural fibers, which we have taken for granted for so long, are seriously competing with and often being replaced by new fibers, dyes, and finishes. These new fibers are called nylon, Dacron, Orlon, Vicara, Dynel, Vinyon, Saran, and others.

These new fibers and blends are woven into fabric used in clothing, draperies, upholstery, carpets, etc. The synthetic fibers offer in varying degrees, economy, lightness of weight, moisture resistance, flexibility, resistance to wrinkling, resistance to mildew, etc. It is estimated that over 90% of women's garments contain synthetic fibers, which are very rapidly invading men's wear as well as general home furnishings.

The appearance of synthetic fibers has made necessary the development of methods for cleaning and spotting them. Fabric tests have also been devised for recognizing them. These are generally discussed along with a brief description of the individual synthetic fibers. Generally, treat synthetic fibers with the same care that is used in cleaning silk and wool. It is often found that they are even more sensitive to heat than the natural fibers.

RAYON

The most commonly used synthetic fiber is rayon. There are three kinds of rayon available which differ in physical and chemical characteristics. One is a cellulose acetate rayon, another is cuprammonium rayon, and the third is a regenerated cellulose rayon which is better known as viscose rayon and was at first popularly known as "artificial silk." Stains do not become as deeply ingrained on any of the three types of rayons as they do on silk or wool and perspiration stains are less damaging.

CUPRAMMONIUM RAYON

This cellulose fiber is frequently found in sheer fabrics and hosiery, and although it has strength, much of it is lost when in a wet condition. A burning test reveals a similar behavior to cotton. Dilute solutions of alkali may be safely used in cleaning, but strong solutions will destroy this fiber. Acids are unsafe to use and long exposure to sunlight will cause injury.

REGENERATED RAYON

This synthetic vegetable fiber includes rayons known as Viscose and Bemberg. Since these fibers lose from 40 to 70% of their strength while wet, the utmost care must be followed when wet-cleaning such fabrics. These fabrics will also chafe more easily than silk or cellulose acetate rayon.

Viscose rayon, popularly known as "Celanese," is an inexpensive fiber, widely used in knit wear and woven goods. Carpets are increasingly found to contain a combination of wool and regenerated rayon

Fibers

which helps to reduce their cost. Being a vegetable fiber, this synthetic fiber is similar in chemical properties to cotton and linen and can be treated like them in stain removal.

The simple burning test is useful in determining the fiber content of your fabric. Regenerated rayons burn much like cotton leaving no ash and giving off the odor of burning wood or paper.

A simple test is tearing a thread apart. Regenerated rayon fibers leave long feathery streamers at each broken end. This is more clearly observed when the fibers are wet. Cotton, however, breaks clean, giving no evidence of streamers.

When dry-cleaning regenerated rayon, do not use strong acids and alkalies. Mild acids or alkalies may be used but the utmost care should be taken to rinse them out thoroughly. This rayon can be treated quite safely with a dilute solution of ammonia water because it is mild and it will evaporate completely. Acetic acid in a mild solution can also be used in comparative safety since it will also evaporate completely from the fabric. Although bleaches affect this fiber similarly to cotton, peroxide of hydrogen and sodium perborate are the safest bleaches to use with rayon. A mild solution of sodium hypochlorite bleach may be used if the precaution is taken to neutralize it following its use.

Regenerated rayon shows resistance to yellowing and perspiration damage and it does not readily absorb most of the common stains. This rayon is often blended with wool in men's suits where it is not easily detected. It is advisable, therefore, to make certain of the fiber content by testing the fabric. The use of alcohol as a stain remover should be avoided as far as possible since it may affect the color of the cloth. Garments frequently contain regenerated rayon with cellulose acetate rayon and since they differ from each other, it is advisable to identify them before using a stain remover.

FORTISAN

This product is made by the same company that manufactures "Celanese." It is a fine-quality regenerated rayon. It is stronger than silk. The same methods of stain removal are used on Fortisan as are used on other regenerated rayon fabrics. A burning test gives the same characteristics as observed with viscose rayon. Other rayons of the same type are Tenasco and Durafil.

CELLULOSE ACETATE RAYON

Cellulose acetate rayon is widely used in all kinds of women's and men's wear, as well as in draperies and upholstery fabrics. It is often used in combination with other fibers to produce new effects and characteristics. A burning test can be made by holding a flame at the very edge of a sample of thread. A melting away of the fiber is observed, leaving shiny black beads of ash which are not easily separated from the unburned fiber. Even when the flame is removed, burning and smouldering continue, and the odor given off is much like that of burning rubber.

Since acetate rayon differs chemically from viscose rayon, many solvents may be used for one but not for the other. Avoid the use of alcohol, acetone, or chloroform because these will dissolve the fiber. A conclusive test for this fiber is the following chemical test. Cut a small sample from your garment and rub acetone into it. The fiber is dissolved, leaving a soft sticky mass. As the acetone evaporates, the cloth will harden. Mixtures containing cellulose acetate rayon should be cleaned as though it were composed only of acetate rayon. Soap and water is a highly effective stain remover for cellulose acetate rayon whenever its use is made possible. Do not use hot iron; it may melt the acetate rayon.

ETHYL CELLULOSE RAYON

A very strong fiber made from ethyl cellulose is sometimes found in lining fabric. It burns like cellulose acetate rayon and is similar in its chemical reactions. It is well to remember that this fiber will dissolve in almost all of the commonly used dry-cleaning solvents. However, Stoddard solvent or V. M. & P. naphtha is safe to use.

PLEXON

This is a viscose rayon that is coated with a plastic to make it stiff enough to be used in making hats, shoes, draperies, and luggage. Acetone will dissolve the plastic coating and before using this solvent make certain that it does not damage your cloth by first making a test on an inconspicuous area.

Since World War II, a great variety of synthetic materials has been made from such protein products as peanuts, corn, soybean, milk, fish, etc. Being protein fibers, these are treated the same as silk or wool when removing stains. Stains are usually easy to remove by soap and water from these fibers.

NYLON

Nylon is the major synthetic fiber in recent years, stimulating the growth of textiles to include the large variety we meet today. It combines sheerness with great strength and durability. It is stronger than any natural fiber and its good flexing qualities, so important in stockings, established it firmly in public favor. Nylon is also made into seat covers, dresses, sweaters, underwear, girdles, bathing suits, snow suits, jackets, rain coats, etc., and blends are found in wool-type fabrics, such as socks, suits, rugs, furs, etc.

Nylon does not dissolve in acetone and it resists the effects of a wide variety of chemicals, acids, and alkalies, thus making spot removal a far simpler task than is usual with other fabrics. Ammonia water, rust removers, and digestive materials are also safely used on nylon. Difficulty is encountered, however, when removing a dyelike stain. Soap and water is a highly favorable means of stain removal whenever it is possible to use it.

The ordinary types of bleaches, especially the chlorine bleaches, do not have any bleaching effect on nylon but the dye of the fabric may be injured when used.

Nylon is highly resistant to moisture and liquid stains, such as fruit juice, tea, coffee, coca cola, and others; they are likely to remain on the surface and are, therefore, easily washed off. This fiber should never be subjected to high temperatures and only a warm iron may be used for pressing.

The burning test reveals that nylon does not burn as easily as do the rayons and when the flame is removed, the burning discontinues. It forms beads that are similar to those formed by cellulose acetate rayon, but they are light tan or white rather than black. The odor of burning nylon is like that of burning sealing wax and in no way can it be mistaken for either burning regenerated rayon or cotton.

With the success of nylon other test-tube fibers came into being which have many characteristics in common, but differ in the degree of flexibility, draping quality, resistance to moisture or wrinkling, resistance to acids, etc., and in washability.

GRILON

Grilon is a new Swiss fiber which is considered to be similar to nylon.

PERLON

Perlon is a German fiber similar to nylon.

ACRILAN (CHEMSTRAND)

This is a new synthetic fiber resembling Orlon.

ORLON

This durable DuPont fiber is made from polyacrylonitrile. It has exceptionally high bulk, but is light in weight and has a wool-like feel. It absorbs little moisture and is, therefore, useful in fabrics made to resist weathering. It is resistant to moths and mildew and it is used for wearing apparel, such as shirts, men's suits, lingerie, and outdoor fabrics, such as awnings, yacht sails, marine uniforms, and others.

DACRON

Dacron is also a DuPont fiber and is chemically a polyester. It is a light, strong fiber, resisting friction and it feels and looks like wool. At room temperature, it responds to weak acid and alkali treatment but hot solutions of acids and alkalies should be avoided. Like nylon, it absorbs very little moisture. It has a higher heat resistance than nylon, doesn't shrink or stretch, and is proof against moths and mildew. It is used for the manufacture of socks, sporting goods, men's suits, and other wearing apparel.

DYNEL

This is an acrylic-vinyl fiber which is wool-like in appearance. Dynel is thermoplastic and has the warmth of wool, is washable, and almost shrinkproof. It will hold a crease even when wet. It is employed increasingly to replace wool for knit goods, underwear, socks, sport goods, etc.

Fibers 19

VICARA

Vicara and other zein fibers, are made from the protein of corn. Because this fiber is made to feel and look like wool having a cashmere-like appearance, it is frequently blended with it, as well as with other fibers, such as rayon, in order to add softness to and increase the draping qualities or flexibility of these fabrics. It is blended with nylon to make nylon water absorbent.

VINYON

This new synthetic fiber is made from mixed vinyls. It resists the effect of acids, alkalies, sunlight, and aging and is woven into fabrics used in upholstery and other home fabrics. It is also found in belts, suspenders, and neckties. Since Vinyon dissolves in acetone and chloroform, test the fabric before using these solvents for stain removing.

Vinyon N

This synthetic fiber is made from a copolymer of vinyl chloride and acrylonitrile. It is considered superior to Vinyon because of its resistance to heat and many organic solvents. It can be safely treated with alkalies and acids, but will dissolve in acetone. In a burning test, it shrinks and hardens without burning.

Vinylon

This new fiber, also made from mixed vinyls, has been developed in Japan where is is used in clothing manufacture. The fabric can be made to appear like silk, cotton, hemp, or wool.

SARAN

This synthetic fiber, made from mixed vinyls, has simliar properties to Vinyon and Vinylon. A burning test produces beads of ash similar to charcoal and the fiber chars and becomes shriveled. Saran, like Vinyon, makes a stiff fabric similar to buckram and is, therefore, used for lampshades, hats, shoes, upholstery, and luggage.

ARALAC

This casein fiber is made from skimmed milk. It resembles wool and is mixed with wool frequently. Aralac, however, can be easily distinguished from wool through a magnifying glass as it does not show the scales which are characteristic of wool. Having no scales, Aralac does not felt as wool does and, therefore, offers an advantage over wool. Since casein fibers will decompose and rot when left wet for a long time, do not expose this fiber to the prolonged effect of moisture.

In a burning test, Aralac will sizzle and burn with a flame that is slight and flickering. It leaves a black ash and gives off an odor of burning hair. Hot alkalies are injurious to this fiber.

LANITAL AND CISALPHA

These casein fibers are of European origin and are similar in properties and uses to the American Aralac. Lanital is an Italian fiber and albuminous stains are difficult to remove from it because the spot remover may dissolve and thus destroy the fiber.

ALGIL

This is a polystyrene fiber which is similar to other members of this class.

FIBERGLASS

This fabric of spun glass is on the market in the form of curtains, draperies, and tablecloths. A burning test reveals its identity by its rapid melting and forming a white ash which is dry and light, powdering easily. Fiberglass, when pressed with a warm iron, shrivels and draws up.

PLASTYLON

This is an Austrian fiber made from glass wool.

ALUMINUM FIBER

This fiber is the result of a search for a metallic cloth that will not tarnish. To increase its nontarnishable characteristics, it is frequently covered with cellulose acetate. This fiber is used in lamé fabrics.

ARDIL

This peanut protein fiber is soft and wool-like in appearance. Although it is distinguished under a magnifying glass from wool by the absence of scales, it will felt when hot substances or a hot iron is used on it. This is caused by a melting together of the fibers.

CHAPTER 3

fabrics

With the blending of fibers, fabrics can be improved and new fabrics created, achieving effects in fabrics for wearing apparel and for home decoration that are well in step with the scientific advances of an atomic age.

The newer fabrics tend to simplify the home cleaner's task because they prevent stains from becoming too readily absorbed. It is nevertheless advisable that the home cleaner, before proceeding with his task, studies his fabric and considers the following questions. Is the texture of the fabric crisp or soft? Is it firm or flimsy? Is it rough or smooth? Is it heavy or light? Is the fabric woven tightly, or loosely twisted, or woven into one of many sheer weaves? The answers to these questions, if taken seriously, can carry one far beyond the information needed by the home cleaner. For our purposes, however, the simplest facts concerning the construction of fabric are given here as a guide to the better understanding of the limits of a cleaning job.

The texture of cloth varies according to the characteristics of the fibers used. The fibers may have been chosen for strength, weight, pliability, elasticity, or for their general appearance. Differences of texture are also achieved by the methods used in fabric construction. The fabric may have been woven, knitted, knotted, as in laces and nets, or braided. A weave may also be a loose or a tight one. Texture is modified also by weighting, loading, sizing, or coating a fabric. A fabric may be preshrunk, or it may be stretched, and care must be taken to prevent shrinking.

Woven fabrics include most of the materials we generally use in clothing, draperies, furniture coverings, etc. These are made by the interlacing of lengthwise threads called warp yarns and threads running from side to side are known as weft yarns. The differences in the tightness of twisted warp and weft threads provide for the varying styles and appearances of fabrics as we find them.

Taffeta

This smooth, crisp fabric is made from silk, acetate rayon or viscose rayon. Some silk taffetas are weighted which shortens the wearing life of the garment and stains may decompose the weighting. Keep well in mind that taffetas must at all times be kept smooth during the cleaning process otherwise permanent wrinkles and even splitting of the fabric may occur. Tapping and a light brushing are a good method of handling this fabric.

Chiffon

This sheer fabric is made of silk, as well as of the rayons, and although it is strong, its sheerness makes excessive mechanical treatment unadvisable. A light tapping is best for this fabric, but brushing should be avoided. Many of the usual stain removers can be used safely. A crinkled crepe chiffon will take water spots and react unfavorably to many spotting aids useful elsewhere. Observe the precaution, therefore, of testing the stain remover before using.

Mousseline de Soie

This silk fabric is very sheer and heavily sized. Its sheerness and its sizing present difficulties that cannot be overcome. Its structure makes any mechanical action impossible and spotting agents are not safe to use. When attempting to clean this fabric, it is advisable to stretch the area involved by means of embroidery hoops.

Pongee, Shantung, Tussah

These fabrics are made from wild silk and are used in home furnishings, women's garments, and in men's suits. Stains are removed by the same methods and agents as used on cultivated silk fabrics. Wetting an area, however, changes its appearance which is remedied by dipping the whole garment in dry cleaning fluid. Rust-removing compounds containing fluorine, may produce light spots.

Satin

This lustrous fabric is made of silk, acetate rayon, viscose rayon, or combinations of these. When removing stains, the greatest difficulties are presented by the tendency of this fabric to chafe when mechanical action is used. Water and some spot removers will soften the fabric to a considerable degree. When working with satin, a tapping motion is preferred to brushing and it is far safer to work on the underside of the fabric.

Satin made from viscose rayon loses its luster when water is applied, leaving a dull surface. Acetate-rayon satin does not become dulled by wetting nor is it as easily damaged by rubbing with cheesecloth as viscose rayon. Nevertheless creasing or pinching should be carefully avoided because this will damage the surface.

Marquisette

This very sheer fabric is made of silk, heavily sized with animal glue and then tightly stretched. It requires the utmost care when removing stains because its weave cannot bear the strain of mechanical action or brushing. The sizing is either dissolved or softened by water, leaving the treated areas limp and shrunken. A tapping action is the best means of treating an area of marquisette, and spot removers should be selected which evaporate quickly or require little or no rinsing. The object here is to do as little damage to the sizing as is possible. To preserve its original appearance, stretch the fabric during the treatment and drying period so that shrinking can be avoided. Embroidery hoops serve well as a means of stretching the fabric.

Crepes

Crepes include a variety of fabrics produced on the principle of shrinking some of the fibers in their composition, or forming the crinkled effect by applying chemicals to parts of the fabric, or by the differences in tension applied to the fibers used in the fabrics. The familiar types of crepes are matelassé, crêpe de chine, flat crepes, and seersucker. These are made in silk, wool, viscose rayon, acetate rayon, and combinations of fibers.

A tapping motion is preferred to more vigorous treatment when removing stains. Extra precaution is necessary when working on rayon crepe while wet, since the fibers are in a weakened state and even tapping must be done as lightly as possible. A brushing action is better tolerated by viscose rayon crepe than by silk crepe.

Moiré

This fabric is known for its watered or frosted appearance. Flowers and special designs are used on some moirés. Although this fabric is made from such fibers as silk, acetate rayon, viscose rayon, and cotton, a permanent design is produced only with acetate rayon or nylon which are melted into the design by the use of heat. Moirés produced from other fibers are sometimes made permanent with a coating of acetate rayon.

Acetate rayon moirés respond well to the usual methods of stain removal, but other moirés, because of their lack of permanence, will lose their designs when moistened. Test your moiré fabric for permanence by the simple means of wetting a seam with water.

A moiré fabric made with a coating of a thermoplastic resin is a newcomer among fabrics. Some dry-cleaning solvents will cause this fabric to stiffen by their chemical effect on the resin coating. Test your cleaning fluid on a small piece of the fabric.

Metallic Cloths

Lamés and metallic cloths contain strips of metal or are coated with a lacquer containing particles of metal. A spot remover for this type of fabric should be selected with care to avoid corrosion or other harm to the metal and to make certain that the lacquer coating will not dissolve. This cloth will not withstand vigorous action as such treatment may break the metal filaments or remove the plating of the metal.

Sequins

Sequins are frequently used on garments as a decoration. They are made from a wide variety of materials, such as plastics, metals, gelatin, etc., and it is rather difficult to clean a garment decorated with sequins. Test your cleaning agents before using them on sequins. Sequins made from certain plastics will dissolve in dry cleaners, others may lose color which runs into the fabric, and some synthetic types will soften and curl. Heat should not be used on sequins made of gelatin or they will melt. Metallic sequins present such difficulties as the possible loss of color and cutting the material with their sharp edges.

Pile Fabrics

These materials can be recognized by their special structure. They consist of a backing material containing a pile which may be in loops or may be cut. By varying the pile in length, various types of fabric are produced. These materials are made from fibers of silk, cotton, viscose rayon, acetate rayon, or mohair, or any two of these may be combined. The different types of pile fabrics have characteristic names, such as transparent velvets, panne velvets, cellulose acetate rayon pile velvets, uncut velvets, crushed velvets, crush-resistant velvets, which are treated with a snythetic resin, plush, suede cloth, duvetyn, and imitation camel's hair. Generally, vigorous action should be avoided on the back of pile fabrics to prevent the possibility of pulling out the pile fibers. After a treatment with stain remover, drying should be accomplished slowly so that the pile can be brushed to hold its original position.

Acetate rayon velvets can only be treated with dry stain removers because wetting causes the pile to lose its original form. It is possible to treat water-soluble stains on this type of velvet by placing an absorbent cloth underneath and spraying the stain cautiously with water and not at too close a range to disturb the pile.

To determine whether or not a velvet contains a crush-resistant dressing, wet an inconspicuous area with water. If the pile remains flat after pressing with a finger, a crush-resistant dressing is indicated.

Imitation camel's hair which resembles camel's hair in appearance, can be identified by examining its knit construction on the reverse side. It is usually composed of two kinds of fibers, containing a nap of either regenerated rayon or wool with the knit back usually made of cotton. The difficulties involved when cleaning this fabric are its tendency to shrink in wet treatment and to lose its shape due to its knit structure.

Suitings

We have long been accustomed to thinking that suitings are made of wool. The modern picture is far more complex, however, as suitings are likely to be made from any existing fabric, such as wool, wool and cotton mixtures, rayons, the newer synthetic fibers, and mixtures of natural and synthetic fibers. The home cleaner is, therefore, forewarned to make a test to learn something about the composition of the cloth.

Vigorous treatment of wool causes felting which results in a shrunken, tough, and leathery appearance. Felting, unfortunately, is a permanent condition and should be avoided.

As in other materials, the weave of a suiting will determine the ease or difficulty with which stains can be removed. The soft woolens are made of short wool fibers as in the flannels, and long, fine wool fibers as in the worsteds, serge, and gaberdine fabrics, which usually have a smooth, hard surface.

Wools, because of their tendency to shed water, are likely to form rings after treatment with stain removers, unless the outer areas are feathered out. These rings are more evident on white or light-colored wools. It is usually necessary to dry clean the whole garment after spotting to give it a uniform appearance.

Spun Rayon

Spun rayon is a familiar suiting fabric, made from short, staple fibers of either acetate or viscose rayon or combinations of the two. Spun rayon owes its popularity to its attractive appearance. However, it may not always clean successfully because it may shrink excessively when washed and it shows a tendency to fray at the seams. The finish of some types of spun rayon often contains a synthetic or natural resin and this may be harmed when removing some kinds of stains, particularly those of protein substances. Although smooth areas will resist vigorous handling, seams, cuffs, and pockets are liable to fray under such treatment. Be sure to feather out the cleaned areas since marks and rings are sometimes difficult to remove.

Beachanese

This is a woven fabric of cellulose acetate rayon, used largely in suits and sport wear. It stands up well against shrinking, stretching, and cleaning processes. The same precautions should be followed as with other cellulose acetate fabric.

Sharkskin

This fabric is made of cellulose acetate rayon and its appearance is hard and smooth. Because of its hard finish, stains and soil are likely to remain on the surface. Seams and raised surfaces need care in handling. Wrinkling and breaks can be avoided by keeping the

Fabrics

fabric smooth at all times. Tapping moderately with a brush is usually safe.

Mohair and Cotton Mixtures

Fabrics composed of mohair and cotton are marketed under different trade names. The mohair content of these fabrics is damaged by chlorine bleaches.

Printed Fabrics

The colors on printed fabric are applied in a number of ways and when they are fast, colors are usually not difficult to clean with spot removers. However, some printed fabric colors may bleed or run and thus tests should be made. Colors may be attacked by stain removers which happen to be also solvents for the colors used in the print.

Coated Fabrics

There are several fabrics which owe their texture to the presence of an applied coating. These fabrics include cire and lacquer-back satins, paper taffeta, and paperized satin. Since the coating may be dissolved or otherwise damaged by solvents and spot cleaners, these must be chosen with care.

KNITTED FABRICS

Bouclé

This fabric is made of viscose rayon with or without wool and owes its appearance to the special knitting process used in its manufacture. It has a rough surface which causes stains to adhere more strongly. Moisture will diminish its luster due to the flattening out of the fibers moistened.

Knitted Wool Fabrics

This type of fabric owes its appearance to loosely spun fibers. The method of stain removal is much the same as used with other woolen fabrics, but its loose weave requires additional care in handling, to prevent breakage of the yarn, and to prevent felting.

Net and Lace

Net is made by twisting and knotting the fibers into the shapes that are familiar in this type of fabric. Lace is also a meshed fabric, but it is constructed into a pattern. Either of these fabrics may be made of silk, rayon, wool, linen or cotton. The fragile structure of lace and net requires the utmost care in handling. The net fabric known as bobbinet contains a sizing which may cause rings and high temperatures will cause yellowing. A tapping action is the advisable treatment rather than a more vigorous one.

CHAPTER 4

dyes

A label often advises the buyer that this or that fabric is fast dyed. Moreover, the careful consumer insists that the color should be fast especially on fabrics used in home furnishings. An elementary presentation of the principles of producing color will help in the understanding of the behavior of textile dyes. All the colors are derived from the primary colors of red, yellow, and blue. By combining two or three of these, any color can be made. A simple example is the combination of yellow and blue to produce green.

This is the method used in producing color in the dying of fabrics, that is, two or three different dyes may be used to form the color desired. There are some chemicals which produce a color directly, others need an additional agent to bring out the color. The chemicals utilized as dyes vary and are classified according to their chemical nature.

Acid Dyes

Most dyes of this group will stand up well to the effects of light. They are applied frequently to lighter-weight wool fabrics used for dresses and suits. Being acid, these dyes are particularly sensitive to perspiration especially at the underarm areas. Perspiration is alkaline and forms a salt with the acid dye. For the same reason, alkaline spotting agents, such as ammonia, soap, etc., should not be used where these dyes are present, or bleeding and change of color will follow.

Basic Dyes

These dyes are recognized by the intensity of their color which is of high brilliancy and beauty. They are often used on silks, viscose rayon, and cotton and are generally applied as a topping. This means that the fabric is dyed first with a dye that adheres firmly to the fiber and the basic dye of a corresponding color is then used over this to give it the brilliance desired. Basic dyes do not hold up as well to light and cannot be as successfully wet-cleaned as acid dyes. Alcohol-containing cleaners will cause these colors to bleed. Chlorinated dry-cleaning solvents will also cause some degree of bleeding.

Direct Dyes

These dyes are in themselves of a distinct color and are used mostly to dye vegetable fibers, including viscose rayon, linen, etc. All these dyes are not equally resistant to the effect of light. Some are excellent in this respect but some direct dyes will bleed in water. The loss of some color when soap solution is used may make little difference in its appearance provided it does not run into a white portion of the garment. Direct dyes may sometimes become lost on garments due to crocking or rubbing.

Substantive Dyes

These dyes are single chemicals used, generally, to dye fabrics containing mixed fibers. They have excellent resistance to light as well as to most cleaning agents used for dry or wet cleaning. Substantive dyes are used for dyeing silk, wool, viscose rayon, and cotton or mixtures of these fibers.

Union Dyes

These are generally mixtures of different dyeing agents combined to dye silk, wool, viscose rayon, and cotton, or any mixture of these fibers, in a single bath. Union dyes are not as resistant to the effect of light as are the substantive dyes.

Vat Dyes

These dyes are generally used for cotton and they are valuable for their excellent resistance to the effect of light, to washing, and to bleaching.

Sulfur Dyes

Like the vat dyes, these are used almost exclusively for dyeing cotton, and their resistance to light is high but less so than that of the vat dyes. These dyes are also sensitive to hypochlorite bleaches.

Acetate Dyes

These have been specially developed for cellulose acetate rayon fibers and, although some are able to dye other fibers, their cost limits their use to acetate rayon dyeing. Acetate rayons are often combined with other fibers, such as cotton, silk, viscose rayon, or wool, and in such a combination the fiber other than the acetate rayon must be dyed separately, the acetate rayon being dyed first.

Alcohol will cause acetate dyes to bleed. Therefore, cleaning solvents used to remove paint, lacquer, and similar substances will injure acetate dyes although the fiber itself is unharmed.

Test Your Color!

This precautionary step is important, not to determine exactly the specific dye contained in the fabric, but rather to discover whether the color will bleed or be destroyed by the cleaning agent used even though this may be otherwise safe to use on the fiber itself.

A simple test can be made on a hidden seam of the garment to be cleaned. Place a white blotter or other absorbent paper suitable for this purpose, underneath the test area. Apply the spotting liquid on the top and then fold the blotter over this and press firmly with your fingers. Look for any bleeding on the blotter and note whether any change of color has occurred in the fabric.

Acid dyes will show bleeding when tested with a few drops of 10% ammonia water. Bleeding may be apparent in testing other dyes, such as the blue and some blacks of acetate dyes.

Direct dyes, when tested with an acid, will change color but will not bleed.

Basic dyes will bleed when tested with an acid spotting agent such as 10% acetic acid solution. To verify this test, you may apply 10% ammonia water which causes the basic dye color to disappear but it is restored again by immediately applying 10% acetic acid solution or any other dilute acid.

There are times when there is no cleaning agent available that may not cause damage to color of the fabric. When this is the case, it is possible to reduce the damage to the minimum by dilution of the solvent sufficiently to make it safe to use on the dye and, at the same time, remove the stain effectively.

By following the simple rule of neutralizing an acid dye with an alkaline spotting agent and correspondingly neutralizing an alkaline dye with a mild acid, colors in garments can often be easily controlled.

Bleaching is often a necessary step in a cleaning process and when applied to white fabrics, it is comparatively safe to use. Colored fabrics present greater risks and a test should be made before attempting the the use of any bleaching agent even as mild as hydrogen peroxide.

Some acetate dyes change color from underarm perspiration. Navy blue may turn red due to the alkalinity of the perspiration. Unless the discoloration is of long standing, the color may often be restored by neutralizing with a dilute solution of 10% acetic acid solution.

Woolen fabric is generally dyed with acid dyes and it, too, will change color due to underarm perspiration. Its color can often be restored by neutralizing with a mild alkali such as 10% ammonia water.

Concerning the behavior of fabrics, only the simplest basic facts have been listed, which should be observed to achieve good results in removing spots from garments.

Two additional essential factors which will determine the success or failure of your stain-removal operations are:

1. Know how to start.
2. Know when to stop.

To assist the cleaner in acquiring this knowledge, solvent action, the purpose of lubrication, chemical, digestive, and mechanical action are explained in the following sections.

CHAPTER 5

basic rules
for stain removal

There are five basic methods of spot removal. It may sometimes be necessary to use only one of these methods. In other cases, all five methods may have to be applied at one time, or some combination of several of these methods may be required.

Mechanical Action

By brushing or rubbing with a brush or spatula, many stains on the surface of the fabric can be entirely removed or, if the stains are more deeply imbedded, can be sufficiently broken up to permit the solvents to be used to exert their action more freely on every particle of stain. The stains which are more likely to respond to mechanical action are those caused by mud, soil, food, and some blood stains. Food has been estimated to cause about 90% of the stains.

Chemical Action

Some stains such as iodine, rust, ink, dyestuffs, etc., will not respond to any other than chemical treatment. To remove these stains they have to be treated with an agent that will form a new and soluble substance with the stain which can be washed out. Examples: Hydrofluoric acid forms a soluble, colorless salt with a rust stain, which is easily washed out; hydrosulfite applied to dyestuffs forms colorless compounds; and when ammonia and iodine combine, a colorless, soluble ammonium iodide is formed. A highly recommended practice is to wet out the stain area to prevent too high a concentration of the chemical used. It is also wise to avoid spreading toward surrounding areas, as far as possible.

Solvent Action

This is the most frequently used method for removing stains. If the nature of the stain is known, a suitable solvent can be selected for its removal. For example, benzene and chlorinated hydro-carbons may be used for removing oil and grease stains.

Softening Action or Lubrication

This method of stain removal gives best results with stains caused by insoluble and inert substances. By applying a softening agent, the particles of stain are made smooth and slippery and are dislodged by this physical action so that they can be easily washed away. When we wash our hands with soap and water, we employ the same lubricating action.

The soap softens and lubricates the insoluble soil on the hands, which is then removed by rinsing with water. The lubricants most frequently used for this operation are glycerin, mineral oil, petrolatum, dry-cleaning soaps, soap solutions, and special detergents.

Digestion or Enzymic Action

This action is similar to the digestion occurring in the stomach where certain enzymes produced in the stomach, act upon the food and convert it into soluble substances easily absorbed by the body. When digestants are used on stains that require them, they convert them into substances soluble in water which are then removed by flushing out with water. There are certain digestants for carbohydrates, such as sugars and starches, and others for protein materials such as milk, albumin, and blood. It is best to use these enzymes in a neutral solution. Cleaners used before, such as soaps, acids, or ammonia, should be washed out before applying a digestant. Allow sufficient time for the digestant to complete its reaction.

CHAPTER 6

safety rules

to insure best results

Cleanliness

The brush, spatula, working area should be clean. After use, the brush should be rinsed well and then hung to dry.

After using water-soluble stain removers, be sure to dry the area before using non-water-soluble solvents when called for in a procedure.

After using solvents other than water, such as V.M.&P. naphtha, permit the area to dry before using solvents which contain water.

Do not use vigorous action with a brush, spatula, or cloth during a stain removing procedure to avoid weakening or otherwise injuring the fabric.

A wet stain should be treated carefully. Avoid scratching or working the stain too strongly, since fabrics are weaker when wet than in a dry state.

A hard stain should be allowed to soften after applying the recommended softening agent. To manipulate a hard stain is to run the risk of breaking the fibers.

Flush out thoroughly one stain remover before applying another. This precaution insures that there will be no unforeseen reaction between substances. Such a reaction may produce a new chemical that may be injurious to the cloth or its color.

Feathering Out

This procedure helps prevent rings from forming after the use of stain removing agents. Start well outside of the treated area and brush lightly toward the center.

CHAPTER 7

equipment aids to stain removal

Good Light
This is a necessity in observing the effectiveness of your cleaning operations.

Tray or Basin
A container is useful to catch washings.

A Clean Smooth Surface
A board, glass, or enamel surface, etc. provides an efficient means of spreading out the stained area.

Spotting Brush
This is particularly useful in loosening and removing particles of stain.

Dye Pads, Dye Pencils, Crayons
These may be resorted to as a means of restoring color.

Magnifying Glass (10 to 20 Magnification)
This helps to identify the cloth, to examine a pretreated stain, and then to observe the progress of stain removal.

Spatula
This is useful in working the stain-removing agent into the stain and for breaking up a stain built up on the surface. It must be used with care, however, since it may injure the fibers of the cloth.

Absorbent Material

Cheesecloth, white blotting paper, paper towels, cleansing tissue, etc., are all useful absorbents and should be placed under the stain as a first step in stain removal. They will absorb excess liquids and prevent spreading to untreated areas.

Bottles

Small bottles with attached droppers and small flexible bottles having squirting equipment, known as aspirators, are useful in holding the various cleaning agents and serve as convenient means of applying them.

Sponge

A sponge is useful in taking up excess liquids.

Electric Fan

Quick drying after a cleaning operation is most desirable. An electric fan will contribute considerably to the success of your cleaning operations.

CHAPTER 8

stain removing agents

The agents listed here for removing stains have been chosen for their relative harmlessness to most fabrics. Nevertheless, all agents should be tested on some unexposed area of the fabric.

These stain removing agents can be prepared by the user or they may be obtained in the drug store, hardware store, or at a cleaners' and dyers' supply house.

Ammonium Hydroxide Solution: Use a 10% solution in a bottle containing a dropper. This can be obtained in a drug store.

Soap-Solution Concentrate: This is a 35% potash coconut-oil liquid soap. It can be obtained in a department store or a cleaners' and dyers' supply house.

Alcohol and Water Mixture: Use a mixture of one cupful of isopropyl alcohol to two or three cupfuls of water.

Glycerin (Glycerol): Warm the glycerin to 120°F. before using. If a thermometer is not available, the glycerin should be somewhat warmer than lukewarm.

Acetic Acid Solution: Use a 10% acetic acid solution. If this dilute acid is not available, use a water-white grade of vinegar, or a 5% solution of citric acid.

Hydrogen Peroxide Solution: Use a 3% hydrogen peroxide solution. If the stain cannot be removed with this, use

Hydrogen Peroxide–Sodium Perborate Solution: This solution can be made by adding one teaspoonful of sodium perborate to one pint of 3% hydrogen peroxide solution. This can be prepared by your druggist.

Mild Tincture of Iodine: Use a bottle with a glass rod.

Hypo Solution (1%): This solution is made by adding one third of a teaspoonful of "Hpyo" crystals (sodium thiosulfate) to a cupful

Stain Removing Agents

of water and stirring until the crystals are dissolved. This can be prepared by your druggist.

V.M.&P. Naphtha: This is obtained from a hardware store or an artists' supply shop.

Dry-Cleaning Soap Solution: This can be obtained in a department store or a cleaners' and dyers' supply house.

Protein Digestant: * This digestive agent can be obtained in small quantities from a cleaners' and dyers' supply house.

Soapless Shampoo: This can be obtained in any department store.

Mineral Oil: ** This can be obtained in a drug store.

Pine Oil: This can be obtained in department stores. Pine oil is used to soften and loosen such stains as paint, varnish, grease, oil, and fat. The loosened stain with the pine oil is flushed out by means of a solvent.

Amyl Acetate: This can be obtained in a cleaners' and dyers' supply house.

Rust Remover: This can be obtained in a cleaners' and dyers' supply house.

Ink Remover: This can be obtained in a drug or department store.

Paint Remover: A solvent-type paint remover can be obtained in a drug or paint store.

Absorbent Powders: Absorbent powders assist in removing by mechanical means a large part of some stains. Examples are starch, chalk, talc (talcum) corn meal, flour, etc. One of these is usually applied to stains caused by grease, paint, ink, dyes, tincture of iodine, etc. The absorbent is applied as a thick paste made with cold water or V.M.&P. naphtha as the procedure dictates. For example, if an iodine solution is spilled accidentally, a thick paste of starch is applied to the stain to take up most of the iodine solution. This paste may be made by adding a little cold water to one half cupful of starch.

When Preparing a Kit: One ounce of each of the following should be used: baking soda; washing soda; commercial bleach.

---

* This is an enzymic agent that is capable of converting insoluble albumin, protein, and starch into water-soluble substances that are easily flushed out of the fabric with water.

CAUTION: This agent is not to be used on fabrics made from casein or protein fibers or on fabrics containing a finish or size consisting of such proteins as casein or a caseinlike substance. It is well to test this agent on an inconspicuous portion of the fabric before. using.

** Petrolatum can be used in place of mineral oil.

CHAPTER 9

stains and methods for their removal

A-1 Sauce. *See* **Meat Sauces.**

Absinthe. *See* **Liquor Stains.**

Accidental Bleeding. *See* **Blood, Fresh.**

Acid, Battery
(Sulfuric Acid; Storage-Battery Acid)

CAUTION: SPEED IS ESSENTIAL! *

Flush out the stain with cold water.** Place a towel or absorbent material underneath to catch the excess moisture. Repeat the flushing with water several times. Apply 10% ammonia water. Rinse out thoroughly with water. Feather out and dry.

---

* Acid is likely to destroy and change the color of the material unless treated in time.

** Should 10% ammonia water not be at hand, immediately neutralize the acid by applying baking soda to both sides of the stain. Rinse with water thoroughly.

Acid Violet Dye. *See* **Stamp-Pad Ink.**

Adhesive Plaster. *See* **Adhesive Tape.**

Adhesive Tape
(Friction Tape; Adhesive Plaster; Rubberized Tape)

Sponge or soak the stain in V.M.&P. naphtha. Loosen the adhesive with a spatula. Flush out with V.M.&P. naphtha. Feather out and dry.*

WASHABLE MATERIAL: Remove the stain as above. Wash in soap and water.

---

* If kerosene is used, flush out with V.M.&P. naphtha.

Aeroplane Glue

CONTENTS: Cellulose ester and a mixture of solvents.

Apply amyl acetate* to the stain. Work the stain gently with a spatula. Flush out with V.M.&P. naphtha. Feather out and dry.

---

*Do not use amyl acetate on cellulose acetate rayon, which dissolves in amyl acetate.

Airplane Dope. *See* **Du Pont Cement.**

Albumin
(Eggs; Blood; Saliva; Ice Cream; Meat Juice; Menstrual Blood; Discharges from Sneezing, Coughing, and Sputum)

Flush out the stain with water. Apply a paste of protein digestant* and permit it to remain for about 30 minutes. Moisten with warm water frequently. Flush out with water. Repeat this procedure if necessary. If a trace of stain is still visible, apply a soap solution containing a few drops of 10% ammonia water. Rinse out thoroughly. Feather out and dry.

WASHABLE MATERIAL: Soak the stain in cold water. Wash with soap and water. If the stain is an old one, soak in water containing 10% ammonia water (one tablespoonful to a gallon of water) or soak in a strong salt solution.**

---

* Protein and carbohydrates respond well to a digestant.

** Stains on silk or wool may often be successfully treated after a cold-water soaking, by sponging with a bleach, such as hydrogen peroxide solution or a solution of hydrogen peroxide containing sodium perborate. Rinse out thoroughly. Test the fabric first for any color change before using a bleach.

Alexander Cocktail. *See* **Eggnog.**

Aligator Pear. *See* **Avocado Pear.**

Alkalies
(Washing Soda; Caustic Soda; Lye; Oakite, Etc.; Ammonia, Trisodium Phosphate; Modified Alkalies; Soda Ash)

CAUTION: Speed in removing the alkali is important since the color or fabric may be injured.*

---

* When the color is entirely or partly destroyed, it may be necessary to redye the garment. A small faded area may be corrected by the use of a dye pad or with a crayon.

Flush out with cold water. Apply a few drops of 10% acetic acid solution.** Flush out with water to remove the acid completely. Feather out and dry.

** Lemon juice or vinegar may be used in place of 10% acetic acid solution. Be sure to rinse out thoroughly.

Aluminum Paint
(Zinc Paint; Aluminum Powder; Zinc Powder; Du Pont Cement; Airplain Dope)

CONTENTS: Powdered aluminum, cellulose gum, drying oils, and solvents.

Apply amyl acetate to the area. Apply a dry-cleaning soap. Loosen the stain with a brush. Flush out with V.M.&P. naphtha. Feather out and dry.

Aluminum Powder. *See* **Aluminum Paint.**

Ammonia. *See* **Alkalies.**

Angostura. *See* **Gin Drinks.**

Aniline Dye Inks. *See* **Red, Green, Violet Inks.**

Animal Glue
SOURCE: Gelatinous substances extracted from the bones of animals and fish, hides, hoofs, etc. These are protein in nature.

Flush out the stain with warm water. Apply a paste of protein digestant and leave it on for about 30 minutes. Moisten frequently with warm water. Flush out with water. Apply a few drops of 10% ammonia water. Loosen the stain with a brush. Flush out with water. Feather out and dry.

WASHABLE MATERIAL: Soak in warm water. If the stain is difficult to remove, soak in warm, soapy water containing a little washing soda. Rinse well.

Animal Stains
These stains are made by household pets and are usually found on rugs, upholstery fabrics, and garments.

CONTENTS: Albuminous material, soluble organic matter, salts, ammonia, and water.

Flush out the stain with water. Apply a few drops of 10% acetic acid solution. Flush out with water. Feather out and dry.

If a trace of the stain remains, apply 3% hydrogen peroxide solution. Flush out with water. Feather out and dry.

Antiperspirants
(Deodorants)

CONTENTS: These may contain an astringent, such as aluminum chloride, some hydrochloric acid, and alcohol in a cold cream * or vanishing cream base.

Apply V.M.&P. naphtha to the stain. Dry. Sponge with water. Apply a soapless shampoo. Flush out with water. Feather out and dry.
WASHABLE MATERIAL: Soak the stain in soapy water containing a little 10% ammonia water and rinse well.

---

* Sometimes the grease spot left by the cream will hide the discoloration or damage done to the fabric.

Apples. *See* **Tannin Stains.**

Argyrol
(Silver Albuminate)

Sponge the area with water. Apply a paste of protein digestant to the stain and leave it on for about 30 minutes. Moisten frequently with warm water. Flush out with water. Apply several drops of a mild tincture of iodine and leave it on for about 15 minutes. Flush out with water. Sponge with a "Hypo" solution. Rinse thoroughly with water. Feather out and dry.

Arnica

SOURCE: Antiseptic dressings.

CONTENTS: Arnica extract, comprising tannin, oil, coloring matter, etc.

Sponge the stain with an alcohol and water mixture. Add a few drops of 10% acetic acid solution. Apply a soapless shampoo. Brush to loosen the stain. Flush out with the alcohol–water mixture. Flush out with water. Feather out and dry.

Artists' Paint

CONTENTS: Pigment ground in oil.

Place an absorbent material under the stain. Apply a dry lubricant, such as a soapless shampoo. Apply V.M.&P. naphtha. Loosen the paint with a brush. Flush out with V.M.&P. naphtha. Feather out and dry.

If a trace of stain is still visible, apply 3% hydrogen peroxide solution. Flush out with water. Feather out and dry.

Asphalt
(Tars; Road Oils; Pitch; Grease; Roofing Compounds)

CONTENTS: A composition of tar, sulfur, carbon, and oil.

Place the stain over an absorbent surface, such as cheesecloth, blotter, etc. Saturate the stain with a lubricant, such as mineral oil* or soapless shampoo. Loosen the stain with a brush. Flush out with V.M.&P. naphtha. Feather out and dry.

WASHABLE MATERIAL: Treat the stain with a lubricant to soften. Then wash with soap and water.

---

* In place of mineral oil, petrolatum may be used as a lubricant.

Astringosol. See **Mouthwash stains.**

Automobile Polishing Waxes. *See* **Beeswax.**

Autopsy Stains. *See* **Embalming Fluid.**

Avocado Pear
(Alligator Pear)

Flush out with water to soften the stain. Dry. Saturate the stain with V.M.&P. naphtha. Loosen the stain with a brush. Flush out with V.M.&P. naphtha. Feather out and dry.

Awning Drippings
(Shed Drippings)

SOURCE: These stains are caused by rain washing down such materials as soot, soil, rust, etc.

Place an absorbent, such as starch, over the stain. Apply a soapless shampoo. Moisten with water. Loosen the stain with a brush. Flush out with water.

If a trace of stain still remains, apply a 3% hydrogen peroxide–sodium perborate solution. Flush out with water. Feather out and dry.*

---

*If an iron rust stain remains, remove as directed under Rust Stain.

Axle Grease *See* **Mineral Oils and Greases.**

Ball-Point-Pen Ink

CONTENTS: Dye, oil, and solvent.

Apply amyl acetate to the stain. Apply a dry-cleaning soap. Flush out with V.M.&P. naphtha. Feather out and dry.

Beef Juice. *See* Meat Juices.

Beer

CONTENTS: Sugar, dextrine, albuminous matter, alcohol, and water.

Sponge the stain with water. Add a few drops of 10% acetic acid solution. Brush to loosen the stain. Flush out with water. Apply a protein digestant. Permit standing for about 30 minutes. Keep moist with warm water. Flush out with water. Feather out and dry.

If a stain is still visible and the cloth permits, apply 3% hydrogen peroxide solution. Flush out with water. Feather out and dry.

Bacon Fat. *See* Cooking Oils and Fats.

Beeswax

This is a wax made by bees and used for building the honeycomb.

Place under and over the stain an absorbent material, such as a blotter, paper towels, Kleenex, etc. Press with a warm iron. If some wax remains, place under the stain a fresh absorbent material, such as a blotter. Sponge with V.M.&P. naphtha. Brush to loosen particles of stain. Flush out with V.M.&P. naphtha. Feather out and dry.

WASHABLE MATERIAL: Scrape off the excess wax with a dull blade. Place the stain between paper towels. Press with a warm iron. Sponge with V.M.&P. naphtha and then wash in soap and water.

Beetroot. *See* **Berry Stains.**

Berry Stains *
(Fruit Stains; Strawberries; Raspberries; Blackberries; Blueberries; Currants; Huckleberries; Loganberries; Mulberries; Serviceberries)

Hold the stained area over a steaming tea kettle. Apply warm glycerin (120°F.). Brush to loosen the stain. Add a soapless shampoo. Flush out with water. Apply a 10% acetic acid solution. Flush out with water.

To remove any remaining trace of stain and if the fabric permits, apply hydrogen peroxide–sodium perborate solution. Rinse out with water. Feather out and dry. Repeat the bleaching if necessary.

WASHABLE MATERIAL: Pour a stream of boiling water from a height of about 3 or 4 feet. If the stain does not disappear completely, dip into a dilute commercial bleach for a minute and rinse thoroughly.

---

* Treat the stain while fresh, if possible.

Beverages and Drinks, Alcoholic or Soft *
(Whisky; Highballs; Cocktails, Etc.; Wines; Soft Drinks; Brandy; Cider)

Sponge the stain with water and then with an alcohol–water mixture. Work glycerin into the stain and leave it on for an hour. Then rinse out with water.

If a stain is still visible, add a few drops of 10% acetic acid solution.** Rinse out thoroughly. Repeat this treatment, if necessary. Apply 10% ammonia water. Flush out with water. Feather out and dry.

If there is a trace of stain, sponge with a 3% hydrogen peroxide solution or hydrogen peroxide–sodium perborate solution and rinse well with water. Feather out and dry.

WASHABLE MATERIAL: Soak the fresh stain in cool water. Wash in warm soap and water. Rinse well.

To remove an old stain, bleach with hydrogen peroxide solution. Rinse well with water.

---

* Stains of liquor and soft drinks may be colorless at first, but aging, heat from pressing, or washing with soap and water, cause brown stains to appear which are difficult to remove. This is due to the presence of a high percentage of tannin. Wine stains usually produce a bluish color and have a high tannin content. The color and fibers of cellulose acetate fabrics are often seriously affected by alcoholic stains.

** Colored fabrics should be tested before using acid or alkali.

Bichloride of Mercury. *See* **Mercury Bichloride.**

Black-Walnut Stains
(Walnut Hulls)

CONTENTS: These stains are composed largely of tannin.

Flush out the stain with water. Apply warm glycerin (120°F.). Brush to loosen the stain. Flush out with water. Sponge with alcohol–water mixture. Flush out with water.

If the stain does not disappear and the fabric permits, bleach with 3% hydrogen peroxide solution. Flush out with water. Feather out and dry.

WASHABLE MATERIAL: Soak the stain in warm, soapy water for a half hour. Rinse well.

If a trace is still visible, bleach with 3% hydrogen peroxide–sodium perborate solution.

Blood, Fresh
(Accidental Bleeding, Nose Bleed, Etc.)

CONTENTS: Haemoglobin, albuminous matter, serum, salts, water, etc.

Moisten the stain with water. Apply a paste of protein digestant * and leave it on for about 30 minutes. Keep moist with warm water. Flush out with water. Feather out and dry.

If a stain still remains, apply V.M.&P. naphtha. Add a soapless shampoo. Flush out with V.M.&P. naphtha. Feather out and dry.

WASHABLE MATERIAL: Sponge or wash in cold or lukewarm water.

AVOID HOT WATER!

If a trace of stain still remains, or if the stain is an old one, wash in warm, soapy water. Soak for 15 minutes in water containing 2 tablespoonfulls of 10% ammonia water to a gallon of water.

If the stain is persistent, sponge with a 3% hydrogen peroxide solution or hydrogen peroxide–sodium perborate solution and rinse thoroughly with water.

On blankets and mattresses stained with blood, apply a thick starch paste. Allow this to dry. Brush away. Several treatments may be necessary.

---

* If the nature of a fabric does not permit the use of protein digestant: Flush out the stain with 10% acetic acid solution, containing a little salt. Tap the stain with a brush. Flush out with water. If a trace of stain remains, apply 3% hydrogen peroxide–sodium perborate solution. Flush out with water. Feather out and dry.

Blue Ink. *See* **Writing Inks.**

Blue-Black Ink. *See* **Writing Inks.**

Blueberries. *See* **Berry Stains**

Bluing *

Wash in warm, soapy water. If the stain is persistent, soak in 10% acetic acid solution. Rinse out with water thoroughly.

---

* Fresh stains will respond well to a cold-water rinse.

Brandy. *See* **Beverages and Drinks, Alcoholic and Soft.**

Bronze Paint. *See* **Bronzing Liquids.**

Bronzing Liquids
(Bronze Paint; Gold Paint)

CONTENTS: A quick-setting plastic base, a solvent, and a metallic powder.

Method 1

Saturate the stain with a dry-cleaning soap. Add amyl acetate. Loosen the stain with a brush. Flush out with V.M.&P. naphtha. Feather out and dry.

Method 2

Apply a paste of amyl acetate and starch. Loosen the stain with a brush. Flush out with V.M.&P. naphtha. Feather out and dry.

Bug-Juice Stains
(Grasshoppers; Other Insects)

Sponge the stain with a 10% acetic acid solution. Loosen the stain with a brush. Flush out with water. Feather out and dry.

Burgundy. *See* **Gin Drinks.**

Cadaver Stains. *See* **Embalming Fluid.**

Candlewax. *See* **Beeswax.**

Candy *

Apply steam to the stain by means of a boiling tea kettle.

---

* For stains caused by chocolate and dyes present in candy, *see* Chocolate or Cocoa Dyes.

Stains and Methods for Their Removal

If this is not possible, sponge the stain with warm water. Apply a soap solution. Remove the candy with a spatula. Flush out well with water. Feather out and dry.

WASHABLE MATERIAL: Wash with warm, soapy water.

Carbon Ink. *See* **India or Drawing Ink.**

Carbon Paper

CONTENTS: A mixture of pigments, oil, dyes, waxes.

Sponge the stain with V.M.&P. naphtha. Apply a dry-cleaning soap Flush out with V.M.&P. naphtha. Feather out and dry.

Caramel

CONTENT: Color of burnt sugar, sugar, alkalies, water.

Sponge with lukewarm water. Apply a soap-solution concentrate. Flush out with water. Feather out and dry.

Casein Paints. *See* **Water-Emulsion Paints.**

Castor Oil

Apply a soapless shampoo and work it into the stain with a brush. Flush out with water. If a trace of stain remains, repeat this procedure. Feather out and dry.

WASHABLE FABRICS: Soak the stain in a soapy solution containing a little 10% ammonia water and rinse well.

Catsup

CONTENTS: Tomatoes, salt, garlic, condiments, vinegar, tannin, and coloring matter, such as cochineal, water, and sugar.

Moisten the stain with warm water. Apply warm glycerin (120°F.). Work the stain with a brush. Flush out with water. Apply a paste of protein digestant and leave it on for 30 minutes. Moisten frequently with warm water. Flush out with water. Feather out and dry.

If a trace of stain is visible, bleach out with a hydrogen peroxide-sodium perborate solution, if the fabric permits.

Caustic Soda. *See* **Alkalies.**

Caviar. *See* **Fish Slime.**

Cellulose Derivatives. *See* **Aluminum Paint.**

Cements

These are adhesives which vary in composition according to their intended use. *See* **Rubber Cement** and **Lacquer.**

Chablis. *See* **Tannin Stains.**

Champagne. *See* **Tannin Stains.**

Chartreuse. *See* **Tannin Stains.**

Cherries. *See* **Fruit Stains.**

Chewing Gum

CONTENTS: Chicle gum, sugar, flavoring.

Soak the stain in V.M.&P. naphtha. Loosen the gum with a spatula. Flush out with V.M.&P. naphtha. Feather out and dry.
WASHABLE MATERIAL: Chill the gum to harden it either with ice or by placing in a refrigerator. Remove the gum with a spatula.

To remove any remaining gum, soak the stain with V.M.&P. naphtha. Remove the dissolved gum. Sponge with fresh V.M.&P. naphtha. Wash the cloth in warm, soapy water.

Chicken Fat. *See* **Cooking Oils and Fats.**

Chinese Mustard. *See* **Mustard Stain.**

Chlorine. *See* **Clorox.**

Chocolate or Cocoa

CONTENTS: Coloring matter, cocoa butter, oil, flavoring, essential oil, mucilaginous matter, starch, sugar.

Sponge the stain with V.M.&P. naphtha to remove grease and fat. Dry. Moisten the stain with water. Loosen the stain by working carefully with a brush. Apply a thick paste of protein digestant and leave it on for about 30 minutes. Moisten frequently with warm water. Flush out with water. Feather out and dry.

To remove any remaining stain, moisten it with water. Apply a few drops of 10% acetic acid solution and work it in carefully with a spatula. Flush out with water. Apply a few drops of 10% ammonia water to neutralize the stain. Add a few drops of a soapless shampoo. Flush out with water. Feather out and dry.

WASHABLE MATERIAL: Wash in warm, soapy water.

To remove a persistant stain, sponge with a hydrogen peroxide solution or with a hydrogen peroxide–sodium perborate solution, if the fabric permits. Rinse out thoroughly with water.

Chromic Acid

This is a chemical used in the tanning industry. Sponge the stain with water. Apply a few drops of 10% ammonia water. Flush out with water. Feather out and dry.

If a trace of stain remains, moisten it with water. Apply a rust remover and leave it on a few minutes. Flush out with water. Feather out and dry.

Cider. *See* **Beverages and Drinks, Alcoholic or Soft.**

Citrus-Fruit Stains *
(Lemons; Oranges; Grapefruit; Limes)

Apply warm glycerin (120°F.). Work it in well with a spatula or brush. Flush out with water. Add a few drops of 10% acetic acid solution. Work in with a brush. Flush out with water.

If a trace of stain remains, bleach with 3% hydrogen peroxide solution, if the fabric permits. Flush out with water. Feather out and dry.

Household linen and cotton can be treated for persistant stains with a commercial bleach. Use 1 teaspoonful to a cup of water and then flush out well with water.

---

* The tannin in old stains makes it more difficult to remove them.

Civet Cat Odor and Stain. *See* **Skunk Odor.**

Clam Juice. *See* **Fish Slime.**

Claret. *See* **Beverages and Drinks, Alcoholic or Soft.**

Clorox
(Chlorine; Other Hypochlorite Bleaches)

The extent of damage done depends on the strength of the bleach solution used, or on the length of time the fabric is exposed to its action. The bleach may either destroy the fiber or the color of the fabric or leave a yellow stain.

Flush out the bleach with generous quantities of water.

Coal Tar. *See* **Pitch.**

Coca Cola

CONTENTS: Coloring matter, flavoring, sugar, tannin, organic extracts, water, etc.

Saturate the stain with warm glycerin (120°F.). Loosen the stain with a brush. Flush out with water. Feather out and dry.

Cocktails. *See* **Beverages and Drinks, Alcoholic and Soft, and Liquor Stains.**

Cocoa. *See* **Chocolate or Cocoa.**

Cod-Liver Oil

This is a fish oil with or without emulsifying agent, albuminous matter, and flavoring.

If the stain is fresh, apply an absorbent powder to it. Brush off. Apply a paste of starch and V.M.&P. naphtha. Flush out with V.M.&P. naphtha. Feather out and dry.

To remove an old stain, apply a lubricant, such as pine oil. Loosen the stain with a brush. Flush out with V.M.&P. naphtha. Feather out and dry.

Coffee and Tea

CONTENTS: Coloring matter, protein, fat, organic acids, dextrins, etc.

These belong to the tannin stains.

WOOL OR SILK CLOTH: Sponge with lukewarm water. Apply warm glycerin (120°F.) and leave it on for 30 minutes. Flush out with water. Feather out and dry.

To remove persistant stains, moisten them with water. Apply a paste of protein digestant and leave it on for 30 minutes. Moisten frequently with warm water. Flush out with water. Feather out and dry.

Stains and Methods for Their Removal 53

WASHABLE MATERIAL: Pour boiling water from a height of 3 or 4 feet. Wash with warm, soapy water. Rinse well.

To remove any remaining stain, sponge with 3% hydrogen peroxide solution or with hydrogen peroxide–sodium perborate solution. Rinse thoroughly with water.

Color Change

Apply 10% acetic acid solution to the faded area and leave it on for 10 minutes. Flush out with water.

If the color is not restored, apply 10% ammonia water solution and leave it on for 10 minutes. Flush out with water. Feather out and dry.

To restore the color, a color pad or crayon may also be applied.

Collodion. *See* **Du Pont Cement.**

Condensed Milk

CONTENTS: Protein, butter fat, milk sugar, organic matter, water, etc.

Moisten the stain with water. Apply a paste of protein digestant and leave it on for about 30 minutes. Keep moist with warm water. Flush out with water. Feather out and dry.

Cooking Oils and Fats
(Cottonseed Oil; Olive Oil; Lard; Bacon Fat; Corn Oil; Hydrogenated Oils, such as Crisco, Etc.; Chicken Fat; Etc.)

Saturate the stain with V.M.&P. naphtha. Loosen the stain with a brush. Flush out with V.M.&P. naphtha. Feather out and dry.

Corn Oil. *See* **Cooking Oils and Fats.**

Corn Removers

CONTENTS: Collodion, organic acids, coloring matter, and solvents.

Sponge the stain with amyl acetate. Loosen the stain with a spatula or brush. Flush out with V.M.&P. naphtha. Feather out and dry.

Corrosion

It consists of greenish stains due to copper or brass.

Apply a soapless shampoo and work it into stain with a brush. Flush out with water. Feather out and dry.

If a trace of stain is visible, apply a rust remover and leave it on for a few minutes. Flush out with water. Feather out and dry.

Cottonseed Oil. *See* **Cooking Oils and Fats..**

Cough Syrup

CONTENTS: Pine tar, menthol, coloring matter, honey, sugar, mucilaginous substance.

Sponge the stain with water to remove the sugar. Apply an alcohol–water mixture and, if the fabric permits, apply a few drops of 10% acetic acid solution. Loosen the stain with a brush. Apply a soapless shampoo. Flush out with water. Feather out and dry.

If a mucilaginous substance is present, moisten the stain with water. Apply a paste of protein digestant and leave it on for about 30 minutes. Keep moist with warm water. Feather out and dry.

Crayon

CONTENTS: Wax, grease, oil, coloring matter.

Saturate the stain with V.M.&P. naphtha. Apply a lubricant, such as pine oil. Flush out with V.M.&P. naphtha. Feather out and dry.

Cream. *See* **Milk or Cream.**

Cream Soups
(White Sauces)

Sponge the stain with water. Dry. Sponge with V.M.&P. naphtha. Feather out and dry.

WASHABLE MATERIAL: Soak in warm, soapy water. Rinse well.

Crème-de-Menthe. *See* **Liquor Stains.**

Creosote

CONTENTS: Yellow coloring matter, oil, and coal tar.

Moisten the stain with V.M.&P. naphtha. Apply a dry-cleaning soap. Loosen the stain with a brush. Flush out with V.M.&P. naphtha. Feather out and dry.

Stains and Methods for Their Removal

Crisco, Etc. *See* **Cooking Oils and Fats, Hydrogenated Oils, and Oils and Greases.**

Crystal Violet Dye. *See* **Stamp-Pad Ink.**

Cup Grease. *See* **Mineral Oils and Greases.**

Curacao. *See* **Liquor Stains.**

Curcuma. *See.* **Turmeric.**

Currants. *See* **Berry Stains.**

Curry. *See* **Turmeric.**

Cuticle Remover

This is a strong solution of alkalies.

Neutralize the stain with 10% acetic acid solution. Make sure the acid solution covers all of the alkali stain. Flush out with water. Feather out and dry.

Deodorants. *See* **Antiperspirants.**

Depilatories

CONTENTS: Sulfides of strontium or thallium mixed with a grease base.

Flush out the stain with V.M.&P. naphtha to remove the grease. Feather out and dry.

To restore the color,* apply 10% acetic acid solution to the stain. Flush out well with water. Feather out and dry.

---

* It is not always certain that the color can be restored. The damage may be too far gone.

Discharges from Sneezing, Coughing, Sputum, and the Reproductive Organs. *See* **Albumin.**

Dissection Stains. *See* **Embalming Fluid.**

Drying Oil. *See* **Aluminum Paint.**

Duco. *See* **Lacquer Stain.**

Duplicator Correction Fluid. *See* **Mimeograph Correction Fluid.**

Du Pont Cement

(Similar Cements; Airplane Dope; Nitrocellulose Cement; Guncotton; Pyroxylin; Collodion)

Apply amyl acetate to the stain.* Loosen the stain with a spatula or brush. Flush out with amyl acetate. Apply V.M.&P. naphtha. Feather out and dry.

---

* Amyl Acetate is a solvent for nitrocellulose and, therefore, a good choice for treating these cement stains. Test the fabric before proceeding to determine its safety.

Dye Stains

CONTENTS: There are aqueous, spirit, and oil-soluble dyes. Their ease of removal depends largely on how fast they are attached to the cloth. Sources of dye stains may be: foods, soft drinks, Easter eggs, shoe polish, hair preparations, indelible pencil, lipstick, rouge, perfume, laboratory chemicals, medicinal products, such as mercurochrome, various writing inks, such as blue, blue-black, red, green, and violet ink, marking inks, stamp-pad inks, printing inks, and typewriter ribbon.

Apply a lubricant, such as a soapless shampoo and leave it on for a few minutes. Flush out with water. Repeat this proceedure until the running of the dye stops. Flush out with water. Sponge with a soap-solution concentrate.

To remove any remaining dye, add 10% ammonia water to the soap-solution concentrate and apply the mixture to the stain. Flush out with water. Feather out and dry.

If bleaching is necessary, apply hydrogen peroxide–sodium perborate solution, if the fabric permits. Flush out with water. Feather out and dry.

WASHABLE MATERIAL: Rinse the stain in lukewarm water. Soaking for about 10 hours may be required. Wash in lukewarm soapy water. Dry in sunlight. The remaining dye will require bleaching.

Dyes of Unknown Origin

Apply pine oil to the stain. Loosen the stain with a brush. Flush out with V.M.&P. naphtha. Feather out and dry.

If a stain still remains, apply a soapless shampoo. Sponge with an alcohol–water mixture, if the fabric permits. Work the stain with a brush. Flush out with the alcohol–water mixture. Feather out and dry.

Easter Egg Dyes. *See* **Dye Stains.**

Egg

CONTENTS: Protein, fat, organic matter, salts, and water.

CAUTION: Do not use hot water! It sets the stain.

Loosen the particles of egg with a spatula. Moisten the stain with water. Apply a paste of protein digestant and leave it on for about 30 minutes. Keep moist with warm water. Flush out with water. Feather out and dry.

WASHABLE MATERIAL: Sponge the stain with cold water. Apply a paste of protein digestant and leave it on for about 30 minutes. Keep moist with warm water. Rinse thoroughly with cold water. Wash in soapy water. Rinse.

Eggnog
(Alexander Cocktail; Tom and Jerry)

CONTENTS: Egg, milk and cream, nutmeg, cinnamon, artificial coloring, and rum.

Moisten the stain with water. Apply a paste of protein digestant and leave it on for about 30 minutes. Keep moist with warm water. Flush out with water. Feather out and dry.

To remove any remaining stain, apply a soapless shampoo. Loosen the stain with a brush. Flush out with water. Feather out and dry.

Embalming Fluid
(Morgue Stains; Post-Mortem Stains; Dissection Stains; Autopsy Stains; Cadaver Stains; Morgue Odor)

Moisten the stain with water. Apply a paste of protein digestant and leave it on for about 30 minutes. Keep moist with warm water. Flush out with water. Feather out and dry.

To remove any remaining stain, apply 3% hydrogen peroxide solution, if the fabric permits. Flush out well with water. Feather out and dry.

Enamel

CONTENTS: Flat paint with resins, gums, and shellac.

Apply a paint remover to the stain. Add a dry-cleaning soap and work it into the stain with a spatula. Flush out with the paint remover. Feather out and dry.

Eye Drops
(Murine)

Moisten the stain with water. Sponge with an alcohol–water mixture, if the fabric permits. Add several drops of 10% acetic acid solution. Loosen the stain with a brush. Flush out with water. Feather out and dry.

Eye Make-Up
(Eyebrow Pencil; Mascara; Eyebrow Dope; Eye Shadow)

CONTENTS: Wax, oil, grease, and coloring matter.

Sponge the stain with V.M.&P. naphtha. Apply a dry-cleaning soap. Loosen the stain with a brush. Flush out with V.M.&P. naphtha. Feather out and dry.

Eye Shadow. *See* **Eye Make-Up.**

Eyebrow Dope. *See* **Eye Make-Up.**

Eyebrow Pencil. *See* **Eye Make-Up.**

Farina. *See* **Food Stains.**

Fingernail Polish

CAUTION: Nail-polish remover must not be used on cloth made from acetate rayon or vinyon.

Apply a dry-cleaning soap to the stain. Apply a few drops of amyl acetate. Rub upward lightly with cheesecloth to pick up the loosened polish. Flush out with V.M.&P. naphtha. Feather out and dry.

To remove any remaining stain and if the fabric permits, sponge with water. Apply hydrogen peroxide–sodium perborate solution. Flush out with water. Feather out and dry.

Stains and Methods for Their Removal 59

Fish Brine. *See* **Fish Slime.**

Fish Eggs. *See* **Fish Slime.**

Fish Glue. *See* **Fish Slime.**

Fish Roe. *See* **Fish Slime.**

Fish Slime
(Fish Glue; Caviar; Fish Brine; Fish Eggs; Fish Roe; Clam Juice; Oyster Juice)

CONTENTS: Albuminous matter, coloring, serum, and water.

Moisten the stain with water. Apply a paste of protein digestant and leave it on for about 30 minutes. Keep moist with warm water. Flush out with water. Feather out and dry.

Flat Paint. *See* **Oil Paint.**

Flavoring Extracts
(Flavoring Liquid)

Apply warm glycerin to the stain (120°F.) and leave it on for about 20 minutes. Loosen the stain with a brush. Flush out with water. Feather out and dry.

To remove a persistant stain, apply an alcohol–water mixture, if the fabric permits. Add a few drops of 10% acetic acid solution. Flush out with water. Feather out and dry.

If a stain still remains, bleaching may be necessary. Apply 3% hydrogen peroxide solution, if the fabric permits. Flush out with water. Feather out and dry.

Flavoring Liquid. *See* **Flavoring Extracts.**

Flea Stains. *See* **Bug-Juice Stains.**

Floor Polishing Waxes. *See* **Beeswax.**

Flower Stains. *See* **Grass Stains.**

Fly Specks

CONTENTS: The excreta of flies containing tannin, organic matter, coloring matter, acids, etc.

Moisten the stain with water. Apply a soapless shampoo. Add a few drops of 10% ammonia water. Loosen the specks with a brush. Flush out with water. Feather out and dry.

Flypaper, Sticky

CONTENTS: Glucose, resin, oil.

Sponge the stain with V.M.&P. naphtha. Feather out and dry.
WASHABLE MATERIAL: Wash in warm, soapy water. Rinse well.

Foliage-Juice Stain. *See* **Juices.**

Food Dyes

Flush out the stain with lukewarm water. Repeat this until no more color can be removed.

To remove any remaining color, apply an alcohol–water mixture, if the fabric permits. Flush out with water.

To remove any remaining stain, apply 3% hydrogen peroxide solution as a bleach, if the fabric permits. Flush out with water. Feather out and dry.

Food Stains

CONTENTS: Fats, oils, sugars, starches, albumin, water, tannin.

Apply a neutral lubricant, such as pine oil. Flush out with water. Apply a paste of protein digestant and leave it on for about 30 minutes. Keep moist with warm water. Flush out with water. Feather out and dry.

If the stain persists, sponge with V.M.&P. naphtha. Apply a drycleaning soap. Flush out with V.M.&P. naphtha. Feather out and dry.
WASHABLE MATERIAL: Soak in soapy water and wash as usual.

French Polish. *See* **Shellac.**

Friction Tape. *See* **Adhesive Tape.**

Fruit Stains
(Peaches; Pears; Cherries; Plums)

Apply warm glycerin (120°F.) to the stain. Add a soapless shampoo. Loosen with a brush. Flush out with water. Feather out and dry.

To remove a remaining stain, apply a few drops of 10% acetic acid solution. Flush out with water. Apply 3% hydrogen peroxide solution, if the fabric permits. Flush out with water. Feather out and dry.

WASHABLE MATERIAL: Stretch the stained area over a bowl. Pour boiling water from a height of 2 to 3 feet on white cotton or linen. Other fabrics: Pour warm water from the same height. Wash in soap and water.

If a stain remains, bleach with 3% hydrogen peroxide solution.

Fruit Stains of Unknown Origin

CONTENTS: Coloring matter, acids, tannin.

Apply warm glycerin (120°F.) to the stain. Loosen the stain with a brush. Apply an alcohol–water mixture, if the fabric permits. Apply a few drops of 10% acetic acid solution. Flush out with water. Feather out and dry.

Fungus Growth. *See* **Mildew.**

Furniture Polish

CONTENTS: Wax, oil, coloring.

Sponge the stain with V.M.&P. naphtha. Apply dry-cleaning soap. Loosen the stain with a brush. Flush out with V.M.&P. naphtha. Feather out and dry.

To remove a persistant stain, moisten with water. Apply a soapless shampoo and work it in with a brush. Flush out with water. Feather out and dry.

Furniture Polishing Waxes. *See* **Furniture Polish.**

Furniture Stain. *See* **Dye Stains.**

Furniture Wax. *See* **Furniture Polish.**

Garden Foliage, Fresh. *See* **Grass Stains.**

Gelatin

CONTENTS: Protein.

Soften the stain with warm water. Scrape away particles with a spatula. Apply a soap-solution concentrate and work it in well with a spatula. Flush out with water. Feather out and dry.

Gin Buck. *See* **Gin Drinks.**

Gin Drinks
(Cocktail Stains; Tom Collins; Martini; Gin Buck; Gin Fizz; Ginger Ale; Burgundy)

CONTENTS: Alcohol, coloring, and flavoring.

Apply warm glycerin to the stain (120°F.) and work it in carefully with a brush. Flush out with water.

If a stain remains, bleach with 3% hydrogen peroxide solution, if the fabric permits. Flush out with water. Feather out and dry.

Gin Fizz. *See* **Gin Drinks.**

Ginger Ale. *See* **Gin Drinks.**

Glucose (Sugar)

Sponge the stain with lukewarm water. Feather out and dry.

Goat's Milk. *See* **Mother's Milk.**

Gold Paint. *See* **Bronzing Liquids.**

Grape-Juice Stains. *See* **Fruit Stains.**

Grapefruit. *See* **Citrus-Fruit Stains.**

Grapefruit-Juice Stains. *See* **Fruit Stains.**

Grass Stains

Method 1

Apply a soapless shampoo. Flush out with water. Feather out and dry.

Method 2

Sponge the stain with an alcohol–water mixture, if the fabric permits. Flush out with water. Feather out and dry.

If the stain persists, bleaching may be required. Apply a hydrogen peroxide–sodium perborate solution, if the fabric permits.

WASHABLE MATERIALS: Wash in warm soapy water. Bleach if necessary.

Grasshoppers. *See* **Bug-Juice Stains.**

Gravy

CONTENTS: Blood, oil, grease, flour, albumin.

Apply starch to the stain to absorb the grease. Brush away. Moisten the stain with water. Apply a soapless shampoo. Add a few drops of 10% ammonia water. Loosen the stain with a brush. Flush out with water.

If the stain is still visible, apply a paste of protein digestant and leave it on for about 30 minutes. Keep moist with warm water. Flush out with water. Feather out and dry.

If a stain still remains, sponge with V.M.&P. naphtha. Feather out and dry.

WASHABLE FABRICS: Soak in warm, soapy water.

CAUTION: Avoid using hot water which will set the stain!

Grease and Oils. *See* **Oil and Grease Stains.**

Green Ink. *See* **Red, Green, Violet Ink.**

Gum. *See* **Chewing Gum.**

Gutter Splashes

CONTENTS: Earth, dirt, oil, water, etc.

Moisten the stain with water. Apply a soapless shampoo. Loosen the stain with a brush. Flush out with water. Feather out and dry.

Hair Dressing

CONTENTS: Water-soluble gummy material, alcohol, perfume, and water.

Moisten the stain with water. Apply a soapless shampoo. Loosen the stain with a brush. Apply a few drops of 10% acetic acid solution. Flush out with water. Feather out and dry.

Hair Dyes

CONTENTS: Dyes, iron salts, tannins, acid, glycerin, and water.

Moisten the stain with water. Apply warm glycerin (120°F.) and work it into the stain with a brush. Flush out with water. Apply a few drops of 10% acetic acid solution. Flush out with water.

If an iron stain remains, apply a rust remover and leave it on for a few minutes. Flush out with water.

If a trace of stain of a bluish color is visible, add a drop of 10% ammonia water. Flush out with water. Feather out and dry.

Hair Oils. *See* **Mineral Oils and Greases.**

Hair Tonic

CONTENTS: Borax, glycerin, alcohol, perfume, etc.

Moisten the stain with water. Add a soapless shampoo. Flush out with water.

If some stain remains, treat with hydrogen peroxide–sodium perborate solution, if the fabric permits. Flush out with water. Feather out and dry.

Hand Lotions

CONTENTS: Gelatinous matter dissolved in water containing perfume, acid, glycerin, etc.

Moisten the stain with water. Apply a soapless shampoo. Loosen the stain with a brush. Flush out with water. Feather out and dry.

Hem Marks

CONTENTS: Soil.

Apply a dry-cleaning soap to the stain, work it in with a brush, and leave it on for about 10 minutes. Flush out with V.M.&P. naphtha. Feather out and dry.

Highballs. *See* **Beverages and Drinks, Alcoholic and Soft and Liquor Stains.**

Honey. *See* **Syrup.**

Horse Slobber

CONTENTS: Saliva containing protein, organic matter, acids, etc.

Sponge the stain with warm water. Apply a paste of protein digestant and leave it on for about 30 minutes. Keep moist with warm water. Flush out with water. Feather out and dry.

If the stain is fresh, sponge it with water. Apply a few drops of 10% ammonia water. Loosen the stain with a spatula. Flush out with water. Feather out and dry.

Huckleberries. *See* **Berry Stains.**

Hydrogen Peroxide

IF STRONG, it may damage both the dyes and the fabrics. FOR ITS TREATMENT, *See* **Clorox.**

Hydrogenated Oils. *See* **Cooking Oils and Fats, Crisco, Etc., and Oils and Greases.**

Hydroquinone Developer. *See* **Pyrogallic Acid.**

Hypochlorite Bleaches. *See* **Clorox.**

Ice Cream

CONTENTS: It may contain chocolate, fruit, egg, cream, milk, sugar, gelatin, and coloring.

Method 1

Sponge the stain with V.M.&P. naphtha and dry.

Method 2

Sponge the stain with cold water. Apply a paste of protein digestant and leave it on for about 30 minutes. Keep moist with warm water. Flush out with water. Feather out and dry.
WASHABLE MATERIAL: Soak the stain in warm, soapy water and rinse well.

Ices. *See* **Sherbets or Ices.**

Indelible Ink or Pencil

CONTENTS: An aniline dye, such as methyl-violet, graphite, clay, gum arabic, resins.

Place paper towels under the stain. Apply warm glycerin (120°F.) and leave it on for about 10 minutes. Apply a soap-solution concentrate. Add a few drops of 10% ammonia water. Loosen the stain with a brush. Flush out with water.

If the stain persists, repeat this procedure, feather out, and dry.

To remove any remaining stain and if the fabric permits, apply 3% hydrogen peroxide solution. Flush out with water. Feather out and dry.

Indelible Pencil. *See* **Indelible Ink or Pencil.**

India or Drawing Ink
(Carbon Ink)

There are two types of India ink: (1) lac type, which contains carbon black, borax, shellac, glycerin, and water; (2) gelatin type, which contains carbon black, gelatin, and water.

LAC TYPE:

Place paper towels under the stain. Apply pine oil. Loosen the stain with a brush. Add a soap-solution concentrate. Apply a few drops of 10% ammonia water. Loosen the stain with a brush. Flush out with water. Repeat the procedure if necessary. Feather out and dry.

GELATIN TYPE:

Moisten the stain with warm water. Add a paste of protein digestant and leave it on for about 30 minutes. Keep moist with warm water. Flush out with water. Feather out and dry.

If a stain still remains, apply a soap-solution concentrate. Add a few drops of 10% ammonia water. Flush out with water. Feather out and dry.

Iodine Stain

Apply a dilute "Hypo" solution and flush out well with water.

If the stain persists, sponge with a mixture of the "Hypo" solution and an alcohol–water mixture. Flush out with water. Feather out and dry.

WASHABLE MATERIALS: Soak the stain in warm, soapy water containing a little washing soda (sodium carbonate). Rinse thoroughly. If a stain remains, sponge it with "Hypo" solution and rinse well with water.

Iron-Rust Stains

Moisten the stain with water. Apply a rust remover, leave it on for about 30 minutes, and work it into the stain with a spatula. Flush out well with water. Feather out and dry.

WASHABLE MATERIAL: Rub in a paste made of table salt and 10% acetic acid and leave it on for about 30 minutes. Rinse well. Repeat this procedure if the stain persists.

Jam and Jelly Stains
(Preserves Stains)

CONTENTS: Preserved fruit, sugar, acids, coloring.

Flush out the stain with water. Apply a soapless shampoo. Loosen the stain with a brush. Add a few drops of 10% acetic acid solution. Flush out with water. Feather out and dry.

To remove a persistant stain and if the fabric permits, bleach with 3% hydrogen peroxide solution. Flush out with water. Feather out and dry.

Jelly Stains. *See* **Jam and Jelly Stains.**

Jeweler's Rouge

Sponge the stain with V.M.&P. naphtha. Apply a dry-cleaning soap and work it into the stain with a brush. Flush out with V.M.&P. naphtha. Feather out and dry.

To remove a trace of remaining stain, moisten the stain with water. Apply a rust remover and leave it on for about 30 minutes. Keep moist with water. Flush out with water. Feather out and dry.

Junket. *See* **Milk or Cream.**

Ketchup. *See* **Catsup.**

Kummel. *See* **Liquor Stains.**

Laboratory Staining Dyes. *See* **Dye Stains.**

Lacquer Stain
(Duco, Etc.)

CONTENTS: Cellulose base, drying oils, resins, and pigments.

Sponge the stain with V.M.&P. naphtha. Apply amyl acetate, if the fabric permits.* Apply a dry-cleaning soap. Loosen the lacquer with a brush or spatula. Flush out with a mixture of amyl acetate and V.M.&P. naphtha. Feather out and dry.

---

* Some woolen fabrics contain cellulose acetate rayon. Test the fabric before using amyl acetate.

Lake Fly Stain See **Fish Slime.**

Lard. See **Cooking Oils and Fats, and Oils and Greases**

Lard Substitutes. See **Oils and Greases.**

Lavoris. See **Mouthwash Stains.**

Lead or Solder

Remove as much as possible of the adhering particles with a sharp knife. Immerse the stain in a shallow dish containing 10% acetic acid solution. Flush out with water. Then apply a soapless shampoo. Loosen the stain with a brush. Flush out with water. Feather out and dry.

Lead-Pencil Marks *

CONTENTS: Graphite.

Try erasing the marks as a first step.

Method 1

Sponge the stains with V.M.&P. naphtha. Apply a dry-cleaning soap as a lubricant. Work the stain with a brush. Flush out with V.M.&P. naphtha. Feather out and dry.

Method 2

Apply a soapless shampoo to the marks. Add a few drops of 10% ammonia water. Flush out with water. Feather out and dry.

WASHABLE MATERIALS: Wash in soapy water and rinse well.

---

* Not indelible pencil marks.

Leaf Stains. *See* **Plant Juices.**

Leather Stains

CONTENTS: Pigments usually having a casein base.

Sponge the stain with V.M.&P. naphtha. Apply a dry-cleaning soap and work it into the stain with a brush. Flush out with V.M.&P. naphtha. Feather out and dry.

Leg Make-Up

CONTENTS: Water-soluble dyes.

Place an absorbent material under the stain. Flush out with water. Apply a soapless shampoo. Flush out with water. Feather out and dry.

Lemons. *See* **Citrus-Fruit Stains.**

Limes. *See* **Citrus-Fruit Stains.**

Linseed Oil

Sponge the stain with V.M.&P. naphtha. Apply a dry-cleaning soap. Flush out with V.M.&P. naphtha. Feather out and dry.

Lipstick Stains

CONTENTS: Fats, oils, waxes, and dyes.

Method 1

Sponge the stain with V.M.&P. naphtha. Apply a dry-cleaning soap. Flush out with V.M.&P. naphtha. Feather out and dry.

Method 2

Lubricate the stain with a soapless shampoo. Apply a few drops of 10% ammonia water. Flush out with water.

If a stain persists, sponge with an acohol–water mixture, if the fabric permits. Flush out with water. Feather out and dry.

WASHABLE MATERIALS: Sponge the stain with V.M.&P. naphtha. Soften the stain with petrolatum or mineral oil. Sponge with V.M.&P. naphtha. Wash in warm, soapy water.

If the stain persists, bleach with 3% hydrogen peroxide solution and rinse well.

Liqueurs. *See* **Liquor Stains.**

Liquor, Fat. *See* **Tannin Stains.**

Liquor Stains
(Whisky; Highballs; Cocktails; Other than Gin Drinks)

CONTENTS: Tannin and alcohol. A heavy dye ring results from the bleeding of the dye.

Sponge the stain with water. Apply warm glycerin (120°F.) and work it in with a brush or spatula. Apply a soapless shampoo. Flush out with water. Feather out and dry.

To remove a persistant stain, apply 3% hydrogen peroxide solution, if the fabric permits. Flush out with water. Feather out and dry.

Litharge Stain

CONTENTS: Lead monoxide and glycerin.

Apply a dry-cleaning soap to the stain. Sponge with V.M.&P. naphtha. Loosen the stain with a spatula. Flush out with V.M.&P. naphtha. Feather out and dry.

Loganberries. *See* **Berry Stains.**

Lugol Solution. *See* **Iodine Stain.**

Lye. *See* **Alkalies.**

Magenta Red Dye. *See* **Stamp-Pad Ink.**

Mahogany Stain. *See* **Wood Stain**

Malted-Milk Stain

CONTENTS: Cream, ice cream, milk, flavoring, egg, etc.

Moisten the stain with water. Apply a paste of protein digestant and leave it on for about 30 minutes. Keep moist with warm water. Flush out with water. Feather out and dry.

If any stain remains, apply a soap-solution concentrate. Add a few drops of 10% ammonia water. Work the stain with a brush or spatula. Flush out with water. Feather out and dry.

Maple Stain. *See* **Wood Stains.**

Marine Glue *See* **Vegetable Glue.**

Marking Inks

CONTENTS: Alcohol-soluble dye, carbon black, resin, and solvents.

Place paper towels under the stain. Saturate the stain with pine oil. Add a dry-cleaning soap. Loosen the stain with a brush. Flush out with V.M.&P. naphtha.

If the stain is still visible, repeat this procedure. Feather out and dry.

Martini. *See* **Gin Drinks.**

Mascara. *See* **Eye Make-Up.**

Mayonnaise and Salad Dressings

CONTENTS: Milk, cream, oils, eggs, water, catsup.

Remove the excess with an absorbent, such as starch. Brush off. Mix the starch with V.M.&P. naphtha. When dry, brush away.

Moisten the stain with water. Apply a soap-solution concentrate. Loosen the stain with a brush. Flush out with water. Feather out and dry.

If the color is injured, apply a few drops of 10% ammonia water. Flush out with water. Feather out and dry.

WASHABLE MATERIAL: Sponge with V.M.&P. naphtha.

If a stain remains, soak in water containing 2 tablespoonfuls of 3% hydrogen peroxide solution to a gallon of water and rinse well.

Meat Juices

CONTENTS: They may contain blood, oil, grease, albumin, and flour.

Moisten the stain with water. Apply a soap-solution concentrate. Add a few drops of 10% ammonia water. Work lightly with a brush to remove particles. Flush out with water.

If a stain persists, apply a paste of protein digestant and leave it on for about 30 minutes. Keep moist with warm water. Flush out with water. Feather out and dry.

Meat Sauces

(Worcestershire Sauce; A-1 Sauce; "57"; Other Spicy Sauces)

CONTENTS: They are high in tannin.

Flush out the stain with water. Apply warm glycerin (120°F.) and work it in with a brush or spatula. Flush out with water. Apply a soapless shampoo. Apply a few drops of 10% acetic acid solution. Flush out with water. Feather out and dry.

Medicated Wines. *See* **Medicine Stains.**

Medicine Stains

Sugar, syrup, gummy substances, alcohol, coloring matter, tannin, iron, etc., are possible ingredients. Unless the ingredients are known, the method is a trial and error one.

Method 1

Moisten the stain with water. Apply warm glycerin (120°F.) and work it in with a brush or spatula. Flush out with water. Apply an alcohol–water mixture, if the fabric permits. Add a few drops of 10% acetic acid solution. Flush out with water.

To remove a persistant stain, apply a soapless shampoo. Apply a few drops of 10% ammonia water. If the color changes, flush out with water. Add a few drops of 10% acetic acid solution. Flush out with water. Feather out and dry.

Method 2

Rub a dry-cleaning soap into the stain. Rinse out with V.M.&P. naphtha. Feather out and dry.

If a rust stain is visible, moisten the stain with water. Apply a rust remover and leave it on for about 30 minutes. Keep moist with water. Flush out with water. Feather out and dry.

WASHABLE MATERIAL: Soak in warm, soapy water and then rinse well.

If a stain remains, bleach with 3% hydrogen peroxide–sodium perborate solution and rinse well.

Menstrual Blood

CONTENTS: Fibrin, albumin, iron, calcium, fat, etc.

Flush out the area with water. Apply a paste of protein digestant and and leave it on for about 30 minutes. Keep moist with warm water. Flush out with water containing a little 10% ammonia water solution. Flush out with water. Bleach with hydrogen peroxide–sodium perborate solution. Flush out thoroughly with water. Feather out and dry.

Mercuric Chloride. *See* **Mercury Bichloride.**

Mercurochrome Stain

This is a dye that is very fast to most fabrics and more fast to animal fibers than to vegetable fibers and still less so to the synthetic fibers. Treatment must be prompt!

Method 1

Apply a soapless shampoo to the stain. Add a few drops of 10% ammonia water and leave it on for 10 minutes. Flush out with water. Repeat this treatment until the dye ceases to bleed. Feather out and dry.

To remove a persistant stain, bleach with 3% hydrogen peroxide solution, if the fabric permits. Flush out with water. Feather out and dry.

Method 2

Sponge the stain with an alcohol–water mixture, if the fabric permits. Apply glycerin. Continue with this treatment until bleeding ceases. Rinse with water.

If the stain persists, apply several drops of 10% acetic acid solution. Flush out with water. Bleaching may be necessary. If the fabric permits, apply hydrogen peroxide–sodium perborate solution. Flush out well with water. Feather out and dry.

Mercury Bichloride
(Mercuric Chloride; Bichloride of Mercury)

SOURCE: Insecticides and antiseptics.

Apply starch to absorb the excess chemical. Saturate the stain with water. Work over the stain with a brush. Flush out well with water. Feather out and dry.

Merthiolate Stain. *See* **Mercurochrome Stain.**

Metal Polish. *See* **Jeweler's Rouge.**

Metal Tarnish. *See* **Metallic Tarnish Stains.**

Metallic-Cloth Tarnish

These cloths are woven with copper filaments plated with gold, silver, chromium, nickel, or tin. Many are coated with lacquer. Green stains are caused by the effect of moisture or perspiration on the copper filaments of the cloth.

Moisten the stain with water. Apply a rust remover and leave it on for 30 minutes. Keep moist with water. Flush out with water. Feather out and dry.

To remove stains not caused by moisture or perspiration, apply V.M.&P. naphtha. Add a dry-cleaning soap and work it in carefully with a brush. Rinse out with V.M.&P. naphtha. Feather out and dry.

Metallic-Tarnish Stains

Apply V.M.&P. naphtha to the stain. Work the stain with a brush. Flush out with V.M.&P. naphtha. Feather out and dry.

Metol-Hydroquinone. *See* **Pyrogallic Acid.**

Microscopic Mounting Medium

CONTENTS: Asphalt, linseed oil, turpentine.

Moisten the area outside of the stain with a soapless shampoo. Sponge the stain with V.M.&P. naphtha. Add a dry-cleaning soap. Loosen the stain with a brush. Flush out with V.M.&P. naphtha. Apply a soapless shampoo. Flush out with water. Feather out and dry.

Mildew

This is a fungus growth. The stain cannot be always removed if it is not fresh. Old stains penetrate the fibers and are difficult or impossible to remove.

Flush out the stain with water. Apply a soapless shampoo. Add a few drops of 10% ammonia water and work it in carefully with a spatula or brush. When the stain has disappeared, flush out with water. Feather out and dry.

If traces of stain are still visible, apply 3% hydrogen peroxide solution, if the fabric permits and leave it on for a few minutes. Flush out with water. Feather out and dry.

WASHABLE MATERIAL: Wash the stains with soap and water. Bleach in the sun or use a chlorine bleach on vegetable fibers. Rinse out well.

Milk or Cream

CONTENTS: Fats, greases, and albumin.

Moisten the stain with warm water. Apply a paste of protein digestant and leave it on for about 30 minutes. Keep moist with warm water. Flush out with water. Feather out and dry.

Mimeograph Correction Fluid
(Duplicator Correction Fluid)

CONTENTS: Gums, resins, pigments or dyes, with or without lacquers.

Place paper towels under the stain. Apply pine oil. Add amyl acetate, if the cloth permits. Loosen the stain with a brush. Flush out with V.M.&P. naphtha. Feather out and dry.

Mineral Oil and Greases
(Axle Grease; Motor Oil; Cup Grease; Petrolatum; Paraffin Oil Salves; Hair Oils)

The mineral oils used for lubricating machinery may contain metal particles from the machinery.*

Method 1

To remove the stain from a large area, place starch on the stain and allow time for absorption. Brush off.

Method 2

Place the stained area between paper towels and press with a warm iron, if the fabric permits.

To remove any remaining stain, sponge with V.M.&P. naphtha. Feather out and dry.

To remove any metallic particles, moisten the stain with water. Apply a rust remover and leave it on for 30 minutes. Keep moist with water. Flush out with water. Feather out and dry.

WASHABLE MATERIAL: Scrape off the excess oil or grease. Rub the stain with pine oil. Add a soapless shampoo.

Repeat the treatment, if necessary, until the stain is removed. Wash in soapy water.

---

* If a rust stain is visible, treat as directed under Rust Stain.

Modified Alkalies. *See* **Alkalies.**

Molasses. *See* **Caramel.**

Morgue Odor. *See* **Embalming Fluid.**

Morgue Stain. *See* **Embalming Fluid.**

Mother's Milk

Stains caused by mother's milk and goat's milk are often more difficult to remove than those caused by cow's milk.

Wet the stain with warm water. Apply a paste of protein digestant and leave it on for 30 to 45 minutes. Keep moist with warm water. Flush out with water. Feather out and dry.

Motor Oil. *See* **Mineral Oil and Greases.**

Mouthwash Stains

TANNIN TYPE: Lavoris, Astringosol, Pepsodent, Etc.

Flush out the stain with water. Apply warm glycerin (120°F.) leave it on for about 30 minutes, and work it in with a brush. Flush out with water. Apply a few drops of 10% acetic acid solution. Flush out with water. Feather out and dry.

Mucilage
(Stationer's Glue)

CONTENTS: It usually contains rice flower, starch, etc., or vegetable gums, such as gum arabic.

Flush out the stain with warm water. Add a few drops of 10% ammonia water. Brush out the loosened particles. Flush out with water. Feather out and dry.

Mucus

SOURCE: Discharges from the mouth and nose.

Moisten the stain with water. Apply a soap-solution concentrate. Add a few drops of 10% ammonia water. Work the stain with a brush or spatula. Flush out with water. Feather out and dry.

To remove a persistant stain, moisten it with warm water. Apply a paste of protein digestant and leave it on for about 30 minutes. Keep moist with warm water. Flush out with water. Feather out and dry.

WASHABLE MATERIAL: Soak the stain in a soapless shampoo. Wash in soap and water. Rinse well.

Mud Stains

Permit the mud to dry. Brush away. Moisten with water. Apply a soap-solution concentrate. Work the stain with a brush. Flush out with water. Feather out and dry.

If a red iron stain remains, moisten it with water. Apply a rust remover and leave it on for 30 minutes. Keep moist with water. Flush out with water. Feather out and dry.

Mulberries. *See* **Berry Stains.**

Murine. *See* **Eye Drops.**

Mustard Stain
(Chinese Mustard)

CONTENTS: Ground mustard seed, salt, spices, coloring matter, turmeric, vinegar, and water.

CAUTION: DO NOT USE ALKALIES!

Apply starch to the stain to take up any excess mustard. Apply warm glycerin (120°F.) and leave it on for 30 minutes. Work the stain with a brush. Flush out with water. Sponge with an alcohol-water mixture, if the fabric permits.

If a stain still remains, apply a soapless shampoo. Add a few drops of 10% acetic acid solution. Work the stain with a brush. Flush out with water. Feather out and dry.

A last trace of stain is removed by bleaching. Apply hydrogen peroxide–sodium perborate solution, if the fabric permits. Flush out with water. Feather out and dry.

WASHABLE MATERIALS: Moisten the stain. Rub glycerin into the stain. Soak in warm, soapy water. Rinse well.

If the stain persists, apply a bleach, such as hydrogen peroxide–sodium perborate solution. Rinse out well.

Nail Polish

CONTENTS: Lacquer diluted with amyl or butyl acetate.

CAUTION: DO NOT USE NAIL POLISH REMOVER! TEST THE FABRIC FOR THE PRESENCE OF CELLULOSE ACETATE.

Apply amyl acetate to the stain. Rub lightly with cheesecloth. Flush out with V.M.&P. naphtha. Feather out and dry.

Nail-Polish Remover

CONTENTS: Acetone and oil.*

Sponge the stain with V.M.&P. naphtha. Feather out and dry.

---

* Acetone will dissolve and destroy the fiber structure of cellulose acetate rayon fabrics and other fibers for which acetone is a solvent.

Nasal Drops. *See* **Nose Drops, Aqueous and Oily.**

New Skin. *See* **Nail Polish.**

Nigrosine Black Dye. *See* **Stamp-Pad Ink.**

Nigrosine Ink. *See* **Red, Green, Violet Inks.**

Nitrocellulose Cement. *See* **Du Pont Cement.**

Nose Bleed. *See* **Blood, Fresh.**

Nose Drops, Aqueous and Oily

OILY DROPS:

Apply starch as an absorbent to the stain. Brush off. Flush out with V.M.&P. naphtha. Feather out and dry.

If the stain persists, moisten it with water. Apply a soapless shampoo. Add a few drops of 10% acetic acid solution. Work the stain with a brush. Flush out with water. Feather out and dry.

AQUEOUS DROPS:

Moisten the stain with water. Add a soap-solution concentrate and work it into the stain with a brush. Flush out with water. Feather out and dry.

Oakite. *See* **Alkalies.**

Oil Paint

CONTENTS: Varnishes, pigment, oil, drier.

CAUTION: TREAT THE STAINS AS SOON AS POSSIBLE!

Remove the excess paint. Sponge the stain with V.M.&P. naphtha. Apply a dry-cleaning soap. Work the stain carefully with a spatula. Apply pine oil. Flush out with V.M.&P. naphtha. Feather out and dry.

WASHABLE MATERIAL: Soften the stain with petrolatum. Sponge the stain with V.M.&P. naphtha. Soak in warm, soapy water containing some 10% ammonia water for about 2 hours. Rinse thoroughly.

Oils and Greases

(Salad Oils; Cooking Oils; Linseed Oil; Cod-Liver Oil; Hydrogenated Oils, such as Crisco; Lard; Lard Substitutes, Etc.)

Oxidation due to aging makes these stains difficult to remove. Sometimes they cannot be removed at all.

Apply a lubricant, such as pine oil, to the stain. Add a dry-cleaning soap and work in well with a spatula. Sponge with V.M.&P. naphtha. Repeat sponging with V.M.&P. naphtha until the stain is removed. Feather out and dry.

WASHABLE MATERIALS: Soften the stain with a soapless shampoo. Wash in soap and water. Rinse well.

OLD STAINS: Soak the stain in a dilute solution of washing soda* for 15 minutes. Wash in soap and water. Rinse well.

---

* Add ¼ cup of washing soda to 1 gallon of water.

Ointments

CONTENTS: Medication in a greasy base.

Sponge the stain with V.M.&P. naphtha. Add a dry-cleaning soap. Loosen the stain with a brush. Flush out with V.M.&P. naphtha. Feather out and dry.

If a stain persists, moisten it with water. Add a soap-solution concentrate. Loosen the stain with a brush. Flush out with water. Feather out and dry.

WASHABLE OINTMENT BASE:

Moisten the stain with water. Apply a soapless shampoo. Loosen the stain with a brush. Flush out with water. Feather out and dry.

Repeat this treatment if necessary.

Olive Oil. *See* **Cooking Oils and Fats.**

Orange Juice. *See* **Citrus-Fruit Stains.**

Oranges. *See* **Citrus-Fruit Stains.**

Oyster Juice. *See* **Fish Slime.**

Paint Enamels. *See* **Oil Paint.**

Paintex. *See* **Water Emulsion Paint.**

Paints. *See* **Oil Paint.**

Paraffin Oil. *See* **Mineral Oil and Greases.**

Peach Stains. *See* **Fruit Stains.**

Pear Stains. *See* **Fruit Stains.**

Perfume Stains

CONTENT: Essential oils, musk, synthetics, alcohol base.

Method 1

Moisten the stain with water. Apply warm glycerin (120°F.). Work the stain with a spatula or brush. Flush out with water.

To remove any remaining stain, apply a few drops of 10% acetic acid solution. Work over the stain with a spatula or brush. Flush out with water. Feather out and dry.

Method 2

If the fabric permits, apply an alcohol–water mixture. If a ring is present, work from the ring toward center. Apply a soapless shampoo. Flush out with water.

Bleaching of a white fabric may be needed. Apply a 3% hydrogen peroxide solution. Flush out with water. Feather out and dry.

Pepsodent. *See* **Mouthwash Stains.**

Permanent-Wave Solution

Some preparations will decolorize the fabric.

IF THE STAIN IS PURPLE:

Moisten it with water. Apply a rust remover and leave it on for 30 minutes. Keep moist with water. Flush out with water. Feather out and dry.

IF THE STAIN IS GUMMY:

Apply warm glycerin (120°F.) to the stain. Add a soapless shampoo and work it into the stain with a brush. Flush out with water. Feather out and dry.

Perspiration Stains *

CONTENTS: They often contain grease, oil, salt, depilatories, deodorants. Perspiration often causes bleeding of the dye of the fabric.

Flush out the stain with water. Apply a soapless shampoo. Add a few drops of 10% ammonia water. The color may sometimes be restored by applying a few drops of 10% acetic acid solution. Flush out with water.

When the odor is persistent, moisten the stain with warm water. Apply a few drops of 10% acetic acid solution. Flush out with water. Apply a paste of prótein digestant and leave it on for 2 hours. Moisten frequently with warm water. Flush out with water. Feather out and dry.

WASHABLE MATERIAL: Soak the stain in water. Wash in soap and water. If bleaching is necessary, apply hydrogen peroxide-sodium perborate solution. Rinse out well.

---

* Perspiration may weaken the fabric and care should be used in removing the stain.

Petrolatum Stains

Apply a paste of starch with V.M.&P. naphtha and let it dry. Brush off. Repeat this procedure until the stain is removed. Sponge with V.M.&P. naphtha. Feather out and dry.

Picric Acid Stain *

Method 1

Moisten the stain with water. Apply an alcohol–water mixture, if the fabric permits. Add a few drops of 10% ammonia water. Work the stain with a brush or spatula. Flush out with water. Feather out and dry.

Method 2

Moisten the stain with water. Apply a few drops of 10% ammonia water. Apply a soapless shampoo. Work the stain with a brush. Flush out with water. Feather out and dry.

---

* This dye is more easily removed when fresh.

Piles-Remedy Stain

CONTENTS: Medicinal substances in an oily ointment base.

Moisten the stain with water. Apply a soapless shampoo. Add a few drops of 10% ammonia water. Work the stain with a brush or spatula. Flush out with water.

If the stain persists, moisten it with warm water. Apply a paste of protein digestant and leave it on for 30 minutes. Keep moist with warm water. Flush out with water. Feather out and dry.

The color may be restored by applying a few drops of 10% acetic acid solution. Flush out with water. Feather out and dry.

Pin Marks

CONTENTS: They often contain iron or copper rust.

Moisten the stain with water. Apply a soap-solution concentrate. Add a few drops of 10% ammonia water. Loosen the stain wtih a brush. Flush out with water. Feather out and dry.

For a reddish stain which may be rust, moisten the stain with water. Apply a rust remover and leave it on for 30 minutes. Keep moist with water. Flush out with water. Feather out and dry.

Pitch

SOURCES: Coal Tar, Tree or Vegetable.

Apply V.M.&P. naphtha. Add a dry-cleaning soap. Loosen the stain with a brush. Flush out with V.M.&P. naphtha. Feather out and dry.

Plant Juices
(Grass; Leaves; Foliage; Fruit; Vegetables)

Sponge the stain with V.M.&P. naphtha. Feather out and dry.

If the stain remains and the fabric permits, sponge with an alcohol–water mixture. Flush out with water. Feather out and dry.

WASHABLE MATERIAL: Soak in warm, soap water containing 1 teaspoonful of 10% ammonia water and rinse well.

If the stain persists, bleach with hydrogen peroxide–sodium perborate solution and rinse well.

Plums. *See* **Fruit Stains.**

Pomade. *See* **Mineral Oil and Greases.**

Post-Mortem Stains. *See* **Embalming Fluid.**

Potassium Permanganate

Flush out with water.

If the color is destroyed, a crayon or a color pad may be used to restore it.

Preserves Stains. *See* **Jam and Jelly Stains.**

Printer's Ink

CONTENTS: Pigment, oil, resin, and solvent.

Place paper towels under the stain. Saturate the stain with pine oil and leave it on for about 10 minutes. Add a dry-cleaning soap. Loosen the stain with a brush. Sponge with V.M.&P. naphtha.

If any trace remains, repeat this procedure. Feather out and dry.

Prophylactics. *See* **Argyrol; Potassium Permanganate;** or **Chlorine,** depending on their type.

Putty

CONTENTS: Oil and whiting.

Apply V.M.&P. naphtha. Add a dry-cleaning soap. Loosen the stain with a brush. Flush out with V.M.&P. naphtha. Feather out and dry.

Pyrogallic Acid

Flush out the stain with water. Wipe up as much as possible of the moisture. Apply warm glycerin (120°F.). Add a soap-solution concentrate and work it in with a brush. Flush out with water. Feather out and dry.

Pyroxylin. *See* **Du Pont Cement.**

Rain Spots

CONTENTS: Soot, soil, etc.

Moisten the stains with water. Apply a soap-solution concentrate. Add a few drops of 10% ammonia water. Flush out with water. Feather out and dry.

Raspberries. *See* **Berry Stains.**

Red, Green, Violet Inks

CONTENTS: Dyes, gum arabic, glycerin, alcohol, and water.

Place paper towels under the stain. Moisten the stain with glycerin and leave it on for about 10 minutes. Apply a soap-solution concentrate. Add a few drops of 10% ammonia water. Loosen the stain with a brush. Flush out with water.

If a stain remains, repeat this procedure. Feather out and dry.

To remove any trace of stain and if the fabric permits, bleach with 3% hydrogen peroxide solution. Flush out with water. Feather out and dry.

Road Oil. *See* **Mineral Oil and Greases.**

Roofing Compounds. *See* **Asphalt.**

Rosin. *See* **Pitch.**

Rouge

CONTENTS: Pigment, dye, oil, and waxes.

Sponge the stain with V.M.&P. naphtha. Apply a dry-cleaning soap. Loosen the stain with a brush. Flush out the stain with V.M.&P. naphtha. Feather out and dry.

If the stain persists, moisten it with water. Apply a soapless shampoo and work it into the stain with a brush. Flush out with water. Feather out and dry.

Rubber. *See* **Rubber Cement.**

Rubber Cement

CONTENTS: Rubber and solvent.

Rub mineral oil into the stain. Sponge the stain with V.M.&P. naphtha. Apply a dry-cleaning soap and work it in with a brush. Flush out with V.M.&P. naphtha. Feather out and dry.

Stains and Methods for Their Removal

Rubberized Tape. *See* **Adhesive Tape.**

Rum. *See* **Whisky and Beverages and Drinks, Alcoholic and Soft.**

Rust Stain. *See* **Iron-Rust Stains.**

Saffron. *See* **Turmeric.**

Salad Dressing

CONTENTS: It may contain egg, cream, lemon juice or vinegar, or catsup.

Method 1

Apply a paste of cornstarch and V.M.&P. naphtha. Brush off when dry. Repeat this procedure until the stain disappears.

Method 2

Sponge the stain with V.M.&P. naphtha. Apply a dry-cleaning soap. Work the stain with a brush. Flush out with V.M.&P. naphtha. Feather out and dry.

If a strain remains, moisten it with warm water. Apply a paste of protein digestant and leave it on for 30 minutes. Keep moist with warm water. Flush out with water. Feather out and dry.

Salad Oils. *See* **Oils and Greases.**

Saliva. *See* **Albumin.**

Salves. *See* **Ointments.**

"57" Sauce. *See* **Meat Sauces.**

Sauterne. *See* **Tannin Stains.**

Scorch Stains

Brush the stain to remove the charred fibers. If the fabric permits; apply a 3% hydrogen peroxide solution. Flush out with water. Repeat this procedure as often as necessary. Feather out and dry.

WASHABLE MATERIAL: Soap in soapy water. Wash and rinse well.

If the stain persists, apply hydrogen peroxide–sodium perborate solution. Rinse out well.

Sealing Wax

Apply V.M.&P. naphtha to the stain to soften the wax. Remove as much wax as possible with a spatula. Saturate the stain with V.M.&P. naphtha. Apply a dry-cleaning soap and work it in with a brush. Flush out with V.M.&P. naphtha. Feather out and dry.

Shellac

CONTENT: A resinous substance dissolved in alcohol.

CAUTION: TEST THE FABRIC AND DYE FOR STABILITY TO ALCOHOL.

Apply a soapless shampoo around the stain to prevent spreading. Apply an alcohol–water mixture. Brush to loosen the shellac. Flush out with the alcohol–water mixture. Flush out with water. Feather out and dry.

If the fabric is cellulose acetate rayon: Sponge the stain with V.M.&P. naphtha. Work the stain with a brush to loosen the particles. Flush out with V.M.&P. naphtha. Feather out and dry.

Sherbets or Ices

CONTENTS: Fruit juice, sugar, egg, water, coloring matter.

Flush out the stain with water. Work the stain with a brush to loosen the particles. Apply a paste of protein digestant and leave it on 30 minutes. Keep moist with warm water. Flush out with water. Feather out and dry.

Shoe Dressings

LIQUID AND PASTE DRESSINGS

Apply mineral oil to the stain to loosen it. Sponge with V.M.&P. naphtha. Feather out and dry.

WOOLEN MATERIAL

Sponge with an alcohol–water mixture. Flush out with water. Feather out and dry.

WHITE DRESSINGS

Sponge the stain with water. Apply a soap-solution concentrate. Flush out with water.

To remove any remaining stain and if the fabric permits, apply hydrogen peroxide–sodium perborate solution. Flush out with water. Feather out and dry.

WASHABLE MATERIAL: Apply a soapless shampoo and rinse well.

Shoe Polish

CONTENTS: Waxes, resins and dyes.

Sponge the stain with V.M.&P. naphtha. Apply a dry-cleaning soap. Flush out with V.M.&P. naphtha. Feather out and dry.

Silver Albuminate. *See* **Argyrol.**

Silver Compounds. *See* **Silver Nitrate.**

Silver Nitrate
(Silver Salts, Silver Compounds)

Flush out with water. Apply several drops of a mild tincture of iodine and leave it on for 1 minute. Flush out with water. Apply a few drops of "Hypo" solution. Add a few drops of 10% ammonia water. Flush out with water. Feather out and dry.

If the stain persists, moisten it with warm water. Apply a paste of protein digestant and leave it on for 30 minutes. Keep moist with warm water. Flush out with water. Feather out and dry.

Silver Salts. *See* **Silver Nitrate.**

Skunk Odor and Stain

Sponge the stain with V.M.&P. naphtha. Apply a dry-cleaning soap. Work the stain with a brush. Flush out with V.M.&P. naphtha. Feather out and dry.

If the odor persists, apply a 3% hydrogen peroxide solution. Flush out with water. Feather out and dry.

WASHABLE MATERIAL: Wash in warm, soapy water. Bleach with hydrogen peroxide–sodium perborate solution. Rinse well.

Smoke Stains

Method 1

Apply a dry-cleaning soap to the stain. Flush out with V.M.&P. naphtha. Feather out and dry.

Method 2

Moisten the stain with water. Apply a soapless shampoo. Flush out with water. Feather out and dry.

Sodium Silicate. *See* **Water Glass.**

Soft Drinks Stain

CONTENTS: Fruit juice, sugar, coloring matter, tannin.

Flush out the stain with water. Apply warm glycerin (120°F.) and work it into stain with a brush or spatula. Flush out with water. Apply a few drops of 10% acetic acid solution. Flush out with water.

If a stain persists, apply a 3% hydrogen peroxide solution, if the fabric permits. Flush out with water. Feather out and dry.

Solder. *See* **Lead or Solder.**

Soluble Blue and Green Dye. *See* **Stamp-Pad Ink.**

Soot Stains

CONTENTS: Carbon, oils, dirt.

Moisten the stain with water. Apply a soapless shampoo. Add a few drops of 10% ammonia water. Work the stain with a brush. Flush out with water. Feather out and dry.

WASHABLE MATERIAL: Wash in warm, soapy water and rinse well.

Stamp-Pad Ink

CONTENT: A solution of dye in water containing a little glycerin.

Moisten the stain with glycerin and work it into the stain with a brush. Apply a soap-solution concentrate. Add a few drops of 10% ammonia water. Flush out with water. Feather out and dry.

If a stain persists and the fabric permits, bleach out with 3% hydrogen peroxide solution. Flush out with water. Feather out and dry.

Starch

CAUTION: AVOID THE USE OF HOT WATER!

Moisten the stain with water. Loosen the stain with a brush. Flush out with water.

If the stain persists, moisten it with warm water. Apply a paste of protein digestant and leave it on for 30 minutes. Keep moist with warm water. Flush out with water. Feather out and dry.

Stationer's Glue. *See* **Mucilage.**

Storage-Battery Acid. *See* **Acid, Battery.**

Stout. *See* **Beer.**

Stove Polish. *See* **Pitch.**

Strawberries. *See* **Berry Stains.**

Sugar. *See* **Glucose.**

Sulfuric Acid. *See* **Acid, Battery.**

Syrup

CONTENT: Sugar, honey, water.

Saturate the stain with lukewarm water. Work lightly with a brush to break up the stain. Flush out with water.

If the stain persists, repeat this treatment. Feather out and dry.

Tannin Stains *

(Source may be Peaches; Pears; Apples; Citrus Fruit; Berries; Wine; Liquor; Leather; Tea; Coffee; Chocolate; Tobacco; Soft Drinks; Beer; Champagne; Grass; Walnut Hulls; Chablis; Chartreuse)

Apply warm glycerine (120°F.) to the stain. Work with a brush to loosen the stain. Flush out with water. Add a few drops of 10% acetic acid solution. Work the stain with a brush. Flush out with water. Feather out and dry.

If a stain remains, moisten it with warm water. Apply a paste of protein digestant ** and leave it on 30 minutes. Keep moist with warm

---

* Tannin stains on protein fibers are more difficult and sometimes impossible to remove. Old stains are more difficult to remove than fresh ones.

** Protein digestant cannot be used on synthetic protein fibers.

water. Flush out with water. Feather out and dry.

If bleaching is necessary, apply 3% hydrogen peroxide solution, if the fabric permits. Flush out with water. Feather out and dry.

Tar Stains. *See* **Pitch.**

Tea Stains

CONTENTS: Coloring matter, tannin, albumin, etc.

Flush out the stain with water. Apply warm glycerin (120°F.) and work it into the stain with a brush. Flush out with water. Apply a few drops of 10% acetic acid solution. Flush out with water.

If a stain persists, bleach with 3% hydrogen peroxide solution, if the fabric permits. Flush out with water. Feather out and dry.

WASHABLE MATERIAL: Stretch the stained area over a bowl. Pour boiling water from a height of 2 to 3 feet. Wash with soap and water.

If any stain remains, bleach.

Tobacco-Juice Stain

Flush out the stain with water. Apply warm glycerin (120°F.). Work the stain with a brush or spatula. Flush out with water. Sponge with an alcohol–water mixture, if the fabric permits. Flush out with water.

If a stain remains, add a few drops of 10% acetic acid solution. Flush out with water. To remove traces of the stain, bleaching may be necessary. Apply hydrogen peroxide–sodium perborate solution, if the fabric permits. Flush out with water. Feather out and dry.

WASHABLE MATERIAL: Sponge with an alcohol–water mixture. Soak in warm, soapy water. Rinse well. Bleach, if necessary.

Tokay. *See* **Tannin Stains.**

Tom and Jerry. *See* **Eggnog.**

Tom Collins. *See* **Gin Drinks.**

Tomato Juice and Catsup

Flush out the stain with water. Apply warm glycerin (120°F.) and work it into the stain with a spatula. Flush out with water.

If a stain remains, apply a soapless shampoo. Add a few drops of 10% acetic acid solution. Flush out with water.

If bleaching is necessary, apply 3% hydrogen peroxide solution, if the fabric permits. Flush out with water. Feather out and dry.

WASHABLE MATERIAL: Sponge the stain with water. Apply warm glycerin (120°F.) and leave it on for 30 minutes. Wash in warm, soapy water. Rinse well.

If the stain persists, bleach with hydrogen peroxide–sodium perborate solution. Rinse well.

Toothpaste and Powder Stains

CONTENTS: Sodium perborate and other oxidizing agents.

Flush out the stain with water. Work the stain with a brush to loosen. Apply a soapless shampoo and work it in with a spatula. Flush out with water. Feather out and dry.

If the color is injured, use a crayon or dye pad to touch up the color.

Treacile. *See* **Caramel.**

Tree-Band Stains

CONTENT: Oil, resin, honey or glucose.

Sponge the stain with V.M.&P. naphtha. Apply a dry-cleaning soap. Flush out with V.M.&P. naphtha. Feather out and dry.

To remove any remaining stain, moisten it with water. Apply a soapless shampoo. Flush out with water. Feather out and dry.

Tree Pitch. *See* **Pitch.**
Trisodium Phosphate. *See* **Alkalies.**

Turmeric
(Curcuma)

Apply warm glycerin (120°F.) to the stain. Work the stain with a brush. Flush out with water. Apply a soap-solution concentrate. Add a few drops of 10% ammonia water. Flush out with water. Feather out and dry.

If the stain persists, add a few drops of 3% hydrogen peroxide solution, if the fabric permits. Flush out with water. Feather out and dry.

Typewriter Ribbon. *See* **Dye Stains.**

Urine Stains

These stains may be acid or alkaline, depending upon their age. Fresh stains are acid; old stains are alkaline.

CONTENTS: Coloring matter, albumin, etc.

Method 1

Flush out the stain with water. Apply 10% ammonia water. Work the stain with a brush. Flush out with water. Apply 10% acetic acid solution and leave it on for 2 to 5 minutes. Flush out well with water.

If a stain persists, apply hydrogen peroxide–sodium perborate solution, if the fabric permits. Flush out with water. Feather out and dry.

Method 2

Flush out the stain with warm water. Apply a paste of protein digestant and leave it on for 30 minutes. Keep moist with warm water. Flush out with water. Feather out and dry.

If the color changes, apply 10% ammonia water. Flush out with water. Feather out and dry.

WASHABLE MATERIAL: Sponge the stain with 10% ammonia water. Rinse well.

If the urine is alkaline, sponge the stain with 10% acetic acid solution. Rinse well. Sponge with salt water (½ cup salt to 1 quart of warm water) and let stand for 15 minutes. Wash out well.

If a stain persists, apply hydrogen peroxide–sodium perborate solution. Rinse well.

Varnish. *See* **Oil Paint.**

Vegetable Dyes. *See* **Dye Stains and Water-Color Stains.**

Vegetable Glue
(Marine Glue)

Flush out the stain with water. Apply a soapless shampoo. Add a few drops of 10% acetic acid solution. Flush out with water.

If the stain is persistent, apply a paste of protein digestant and leave it on for 30 minutes. Keep moist with warm water. Flush out with water. Feather out and dry.

Vegetable-Juice Stains. *See* **Plant Juices.**

Vegetable Pitch. *See* **Pitch.**

Verdigris. *See* **Metallic-Tarnish Stains.**

Vermouth. *See* **Liquor Stains.**

Violet Ink. *See* **Red, Green, Violet Ink.**

Vomit Stains

Remove the vomit from the surface of the stain. Flush out the stain with water. Work it with a brush to dislodge the stain. Apply a paste of protein digestant and leave it on for 30 minutes. Keep moist with warm water. Flush out with water.

If a stain persists, apply a soap-solution concentrate. Add a few drops of 10% ammonia water. Flush out with water. Feather out and dry.

WASHABLE MATERIAL: Remove the excess vomit. Wash in warm, soapy water. Rinse well.

Walnut Hulls. *See* **Black-Walnut Stains.**
Walnut Stain. *See* **Wood Stains.**
Washing Soda. *See* **Alkalies.**

Water-Color Stains

Flush out the stain with water. Apply a soap-solution concentrate. Work the stain with a spatula. Flush out with water.

If a stain is still visible, apply 3% hydrogen peroxide solution, if the fabric permits. Flush out with water. Feather out and dry.

Water Emulsion Paints
(Casein Paints; Water-Soluble Paints; Paintex)

Moisten the stain with water. Apply a soapless shampoo. Work the stain with a brush. Flush out with water. Feather out and dry.

If a stain still remains, moisten it with warm water. Apply a paste of protein digestant and leave it on for 30 minutes. Keep moist with warm water. Flush out with water. Feather out and dry.

Water Glass
(Sodium Silicate)

This is a strongly alkaline chemical. It may destroy both the fabric and the color.

Soak the stain in warm water containing a few drops of 10% acetic acid solution for several hours. Flush out with water.

If a stain is still visible, repeat the soaking in warm water and 10% acetic acid solution. Feather out and dry.

Water Marks. *See* **Water Spots.**

Water Spots

Injury may be caused either by the sizing in the cloth having been dissolved, or some of the fibers having become shrunken, or as in satin, by the disappearance of luster.

Method 1

Rub lightly with a fingernail or the edge of a coin over the spots. Iron with a damp cloth.

Method 2

Lightly dampen the spots either by sponging or by holding the stains over a jet of steam from a boiling tea kettle. Feather out. Iron while damp.

To restore the luster, stretch the stain on a flat surface and permit drying uniformly.

If possible, moisten the entire garment.

Watermelon Stains

Flush out the stains with water. Apply a few drops of 10% acetic acid solution. Work with a brush. Flush out with water.

If a stain is still visible, bleach with 3% hydrogen peroxide solution, if the fabric permits. Flush out with water. Feather out and dry.

Water-Soluble Paints. *See* **Water Emulsion Paints.**

Waxes, Colored

Remove the excess wax with a dull implement Place the stain between white paper towels or other absorbent paper. Press with a warm iron. Remove the soiled paper immediately. Repeat if necessary.

To remove any remaining stain, sponge it with V.M.&P. naphtha.

If a color still remains, sponge with an alcohol–water mixture, if the fabric permits. Flush out with water. Feather out and dry.

WASHABLE MATERIAL: Sponge with V.M.&P. naphtha. Wash in soap and water. Rinse well.

Stains and Methods for Their Removal 95

Whisky. *See* **Beverages and Drinks, Alcoholic and Soft,** and **Liquor Stains.**

White Sauces. *See* **Cream Soups.**

Wine. *See* **Tannin Stains.**

Wood Stains
(Mahogany Stain; Walnut Stain; Maple Stain)

CONTENT: Pigments or dyes, oil, resin.

Place paper towels under the stain. Moisten the stain with pine oil and leave it on for 10 minutes. Apply a dry-cleaning soap. Brush to loosen the stain. Flush out with V.M.&P. naphtha. Repeat this procedure if necessary. Feather out and dry.

Worcestershire Sauce. *See* **Meat Sauces.**

Writing Ink
(Blue Ink; Blue-Black Ink)

CONTENTS: Iron tannates, tannin, dye, gum arabic, and water.

Place paper towels under the stain. Moisten the stain with warm glycerin (120°F.) and leave it on for about 10 minutes. Apply a soapless shampoo. Brush to loosen the stain. Flush out with water. Repeat this procedure until all the ink is removed.

To remove the iron stain, moisten with warm water. Apply a rust remover and leave it on for about 30 minutes. Keep moist with warm water. Flush out with water. Feather out and dry.

To remove any trace of stain and if the fabric permits, bleach with 3% hydrogen peroxide solution. Flush out with water. Feather out and dry.

Zinc Oxide Ointment Stain

Sponge the stain with V.M.&P. naphtha. Apply a dry-cleaning soap. Work the stain with a brush. Flush out with V.M.&P. naphtha. Repeat this procedure until the stain disappears. Feather out and dry.

Zinc Paint. *See* **Aluminum Paint.**

Zinc Powder. *See* **Aluminum Paint.**

Zonite (antiseptic). *See* **Clorox.**

www.ingramcontent.com/pod-product-compliance
Lightning Source LLC
Chambersburg PA
CBHW061420300426
44114CB00015B/2013